WHEN THE DRUG WAR HITS HOME

WHEN THE DRUG WAR HITS HOME

*Healing the Family
Torn Apart by
Teenage Drug Abuse*

SECOND EDITION

Laura Stamper

Fairview Press   Minneapolis

Published by Fairview Press, 2450 Riverside Avenue, Minneapolis, MN 55454.

Library of Congress Cataloging-in-Publication Data
Stamper, Laura.
    When the drug war hits home: healing the
    family torn apart by teenage drug abuse/Laura
    Stamper. -- 2nd ed.
       p.   cm.
    ISBN 1-57749-051-7 (alk. paper)
    1. Youth--Drug use--United States. 2. Teenagers--
    Drug use--United States. 3. Drug abuse--United
    States. I. Title.
    HV5824.Y68S77   1997
    362.29'13--DC21   97-18752
                                  CIP

SECOND EDITION
First Printing: May 1997

Printed in the United States of America

Cover design: Barry Littmann

Publisher's Note: Fairview Press publishes books and other materials related to the subjects of social and family issues. Its publications, including *When the Drug War Hits Home*, do not necessarily reflect the philosophy of the Fairview Health Services or its treatment programs.

For a free current catalog of Fairview Press titles, please call this toll-free number: 1-800-544-8207.

To Charles and Preston, who are my inspiration.

There are many people who gave of their time to guide me through the creation of this book. I wish to offer special gratitude to Bob for his patience and help, and to Roseanne and Jude for their encouragement.

Contents

Foreword

Since I wrote this book, much has happened. A lot can occur in five years. I used to half-jokingly say that I didn't want to be working with adolescents when my child became a teenager. The universe must have heard me, because at about the time this book went to press, my Higher Power and my guardian angels saw fit to turn my life upside down by pushing me headlong into a career change. Everything happens for a reason. If we are patient and pay attention to the events in our lives, we actually might learn something.

In the mid-eighties, the health care system began to undergo dramatic changes. Managed health care was introduced. The concept and execution of this new wave in health care was necessary to reduce waste in the medical field.

Unfortunately, while cutting the fat from health care, some of the quality of patient care was sacrificed. The field of treating alcohol and drug abuse, like all other areas of health care, was greatly modified. Patient stays were shortened and the structure of care was loosened. Some of these changes were needed to contain cost. Unfortunately, this practice also created large holes in the safety net, and many people fell through without receiving the kind of treatment they need and deserve. Sadly, this problem continues.

In the late eighties, the treatment program I had worked for began to feel the effects of the budget crunch. Insurance companies made it more difficult for people to access treatment. The first round of layoffs started in 1991, which began a process of downsizing that would change the face of alcohol and drug treatment. My position as open treatment manager was among the first to be eliminated. I had known for some time before I was laid off that I wanted to get out of human services and pursue my life-long passion—art. I was able to do this with the severance package I received from the hospital.

In the last five years, I have had to apply some of what I had been telling parents in the professional setting. Raising a teenager in today's world is not an easy thing to do. I had known this on a cognitive level for a long time, but there is nothing like personal experience to drive a point home!

The first half of this decade has been an

incredible growing experience for me. I have reevaluated some of my past beliefs, and have looked at my own experiences in a different light. My work as an artist has been a respite for me. My career change has allowed me to be home more and to be more available when I am at home. I have gained a new level of empathy for the trials of parenting. Have I mentioned that raising an adolescent in today's world is tough?

When my publisher approached me to update this book, I had to laugh to myself. Five years ago when I first attacked the subject of teenage drug abuse, I based my opinions on my own experience as an adolescent, a drug abuser, and my background as a counselor. Now fortune has blessed me with a new perspective. Being the parent of an adolescent in these troubled times is an endless source of new knowledge.

I still maintain that there are no recipes to follow, that there are no guarantees, and that different people respond in different ways to different situations. But more than ever, I believe that who we are and what we do as parents has a great influence on the lives of our children. I hope that this book speaks to you in an affirming way. I hope that you find a sense of empowerment and a release from problems, but most of all, I hope that you find out that you are not alone.

Introduction

Kids abuse drugs because they are trying to survive. Kids are not criminals, they are not wicked, and they are not evil. So when we fight the war on drugs, we must remember that the drug abusers are often our own children. This book will explore the common issues surrounding teenage drug abuse, treatment, and recovery. It will also help you maintain a sense of order as you fight the war that has invaded your home.

There are no easy solutions to the teenage drug problem. You can't follow simple directions to ensure a smooth journey through life. It is especially hard to present a recipe for raising adolescents.

The most important parenting rule is simple: Do what you need to do so you can feel good about yourself and your life. I do not present any absolutes in this book. There are none. My intention is not to preach or judge. Much of what I share in this book is constructed from my personal experiences as a woman, mother, counselor, and a survivor of adolescent drug abuse.

The stories in this book are composites of the many kids and families I have had the privilege to work with over the years. Having been a clinician, I believe in honoring the confidentiality of the therapeutic environment. By using composite characters, I can more accurately describe the problems that surface in families experiencing chemical abuse. But most importantly, it is the stories that give this book life, because they are about struggling in a world that sometimes makes survival difficult. Take what applies to you and leave the rest.

I have a tremendous respect for young people. Without them, this book would not be possible. Being a part of their lives, I have learned at least as much from them—if not more—than they learned from me. They have taught me the most important lessons of all: compassion, patience, fear, hope, and the need for survival.

No one can deny that teenage drug abuse has hit epidemic proportions. The media has covered the drug war at our nation's borders and through the eyes of the DEA (Drug Enforcement Agency). Politicians have advocated policies ranging from tougher drug laws and mandatory sentences to telling kids to "Just Say No." We have seen movies that point an accusing finger at both parents and school systems. We have followed provocative news stories that highlight a new and menacing drug each season. Hearing about designer drugs or the resurgence of the popularity of heroine can distract us from the real problem, which is that abuse of drugs of all kinds is on the rise among our young people.

One alarming fact is the average age at which kids start using drugs. In the late 1970s, kids began using drugs around fourteen years old. Now kids begin to get high at age ten or younger. With all the anti-drug policies, drug education, and prevention programs, why has this happened?

There is no single answer. Blaming parents, schools, laws, or even the chemicals themselves is futile and exhausting. By declaring a war on drugs, we name an enemy. But are the drugs themselves the enemy? I don't think so.

Mood-altering substances have been around for a very long time. They are inanimate objects that can be used responsibly by some and obsessively by others. If we destroy one drug, another will take its place.

Are the drug dealers the enemy? Many of us would like to believe so. But drug dealers are in the business only because there is a demand in the marketplace. And although drug abusers are being treated more and more like the enemy, they shouldn't be attacked—especially when they are kids.

To win the drug war, we must first stop trying to name an enemy. Drug abuse affects real people on a personal level—real people like ourselves, our kids, and the kids next door. When the drug war hits home, these real people get hurt. The focus needs to shift from being "against drugs" to being "for kids."

Instead of talking about tougher laws and more jail time for drug abusers, it's time to take a look at why these problems exist. No amount of legislation will address why people get high. We need to stop fighting the war with guns and cops and start fighting for the rights of kids and their families.

In all the years I worked with kids in treatment, I never met one who planned to let his or her drug use get out of control. Most kids can remember a time when they were younger and vowed never to do drugs. Yet over and over the story is the same. What started out as experimental use soon took over their entire lifestyle. That doesn't mean every kid who experiments with alcohol or drugs winds up chemically dependent. But too often the chemicals end up controlling the kids.

Chapter One

Why Do Kids Use Drugs?

Parents and concerned adults wonder how their child could have become a drug abuser. It's as if we believe that drug abuse is like a leaky roof. If we could somehow find the bad shingles, we could rip them out and repair the problem.

Unfortunately, it's not that easy. There really isn't a single sign that determines who will be chemically dependent or why. But to understand adolescent drug abuse, we must first have an understanding of what a normal adolescent is.

The teenage years are a time of constant change and turmoil. During these years, kids are struggling to form their self-identity. They wrestle with the values they grew up with and the ever-changing values of society. Their bodies are in a state of metamorphosis, and their hormone changes make them moody and unpredictable. They are typically self-centered and self-conscious. The added pressures of having the "right look" (whatever that may be) only adds to their already shaky sense of self.

Other pressures that kids contend with include:

- fitting into a peer group
- pleasing parents while being torn by feelings of wanting to separate from them
- social problems (including HIV, war, environmental issues, poverty, abuse, and violence)

With all the pressures and anxieties kids face today, chemical use can offer easy solutions. Using alcohol or drugs provides kids with a social outlet: a coping mechanism to deal with painful feelings, a confidence builder, an automatic peer group—and most importantly, it gives kids an instant identity. When young people adopt the identity of a "user," they abandon the difficult process of figuring out who they are going to be. Chemicals provide kids with an instant sense of self. When they get high, they assume an identity—they become part of the drug-using culture. Kids can measure who they are by how much they use and who they become when they are high. In a sense, chemicals temporarily help kids solve problems. Because adolescents tend to live in the present, they do not believe they can be harmed by consequences.

Jo

When I was little, I never thought I would use drugs. I used to think that people who drank and did drugs were bad. Then some of my friends started to get high and I felt kind of left out. I was twelve, and to be honest, I was curious, too. I wanted to know what was so great about being loaded. I decided that trying it just once wouldn't hurt. So I bought a couple of joints and went down by the railroad tracks and smoked them both.

At first, I didn't think anything was going to happen. Then all of a sudden—WHAM!—I was high. Everything looked and sounded so different, and I felt great! I walked around for a while just looking at the trees and listening to the wind and the birds. Then I went home and watched Gilligan's Island on T.V. It was so funny! Anyway, nothing really happened to me. Later, I thought, hey, maybe this stuff isn't so bad after all. After that, I began to use with my friends and go to parties.

For a long time, it seemed pretty cool, except that I had to lie to my parents about what I was doing. A few months later I started to skip school to get high. I told myself that was no big deal, either. Everybody skipped school. School was boring, anyway. Then I started getting into fights with my parents. They would worry that I was staying out too late. I would get mad at them and tell them they were too strict. I would lay this guilt trip on them and tell them that if they really cared about me, they would just let me grow up on my own. I think they believed me because they backed off.

After a while, I stopped doing the other things that I used to do, like playing baseball and stuff. Getting high was the only thing I looked forward to. I was using drugs almost every day, and it was getting sort of expensive. So I started to steal from my family. At first I only took change. Then I got braver and I'd take $5 or $10 at a time. After a while I figured that I could rip off other people, too.

I was fourteen the first time I got arrested for shoplifting and possession. My parents were really upset and tried to stop me from hanging out with my friends. That really scared me. I didn't know where else I'd fit in. It had been so long since I'd done anything fun without getting high. I didn't feel like I'd have any friends if I stopped hanging out with my drug-using friends. So I kept using and things kept getting worse—only I couldn't see it happening. All I could see were the good times.

Everything was falling apart around me—my family, my school work, problems with the law—but it didn't seem to matter. The only thing that mattered was getting high and sticking with the friends who got high with me.

◆◆◆

When kids start to use drugs, they do so innocently. They are mostly curious and usually cautious. They are experimenting with something new and exciting, and in the early stages, without any negative effects. Because they don't experience harmful consequences, they begin to question all the scary stories about chemicals that they have heard.

For many kids, the negative effects of drug use do not occur until they have already had many positive experiences. By then they have already invested themselves in a drug-oriented lifestyle and identity. The consequences do not outweigh the things they enjoy about using drugs.

The major goal of adolescent development is to form an identity. Getting high offers young people an immediate peer group—a way to "fit in." Since drug use offers the teenager an instant sense of self, is it any wonder so many adolescents turn to drugs to answer the question, "Who am I?"

Developmentally, adolescents are concrete in their thinking. They see life in black-and-white terms, and they tend to be idealistic rather than realistic. They live in the present—immediate gratification is more real to them than long-term planning. Teens also tend to see themselves as immortal. Thrill-seeking or living on the edge has a strong appeal for many. Because they are grappling with their value system, they often need to test the limits of the environment in which they were raised.

Adolescent Development:
Peter Pan vs. Mahatma Gandhi

To further understand the problem of adolescent drug abuse, we must take a closer look at the trials of adolescence. Personally, I spent ten years as an adolescent. I survived, but I think I am still recovering from that experience. For me, those turbulent, unpredictable years began when I was twelve. I did not begin to emerge as an adult until my son was born when I was twenty-two years old. I struggled to figure out who I was, and I went through many phases in that process—including a destructive relationship with chemicals.

Today it is not uncommon to consider someone as old as twenty-four still in the "adolescent phase" of development. The term "young adult" is sometimes used to describe someone in their early twenties who has not yet matured.

The time between childhood and adulthood is unique. Although it is a time when young people are beginning to form an adult identity, it is improper to think of adolescence merely as a stepping stone to adulthood.

Erik Erickson, a leader in the study of childhood and human development, pays close attention to this period of life. According to Erickson, we must reach certain emotional milestones before we can pass into the next stage of personality development. These milestones include forming a more solid identity for adulthood. The big question that kids have in this phase is, "Who am I?" If the identity issues are not addressed, the young person will be void of solid values or a stable identity as an adult.

Adolescents are idealistic and acutely aware of social problems (like Gandhi). Yet they are self-involved and resistant to change (like Peter Pan). They see life in terms of absolutes. They can be moody, judgmental, and extremely biased. Yet they are often arrogant in their own sense of self-righteousness. One minute they are full of awe and excitement for all that life can hold, and the next minute they are cynical, pessimistic, and filled with self-doubt. But this is the way they are supposed to be. This is really what those turbulent years are all about.

Chemicals neatly ease all these painful struggles because they come complete with a peer group, their own set of rules and values, and an automatic identity. The identity issues are resolved merely by getting high.

Although this stage of life has crucial milestones, it is unfortunate that it lasts so long, and seems to get a little longer with the passing of each generation.

During the last four generations, there has been a significant change in the time it takes to complete adolescence. In the past, the period of time between childhood and adulthood was as short as one month or as long as three years. Young people would be given clear lessons in their roles as adults during this time. They were taught these roles by their parents, spiritual leaders, and community elders. During the 1800s, young women were often married within six months to a year after the onset of menstruation (which usually occurred around the age of fifteen). This event classified them as adults. Young men were groomed for adulthood by learning a trade around the age of thirteen. Within a few years they would be pushed into adulthood as they went out on their own. In native cultures, at the time of puberty, boys and girls would be involved in a ritual that would culminate in a ceremony recognizing them as adults. In both types of cultures, adolescence was relatively short.

Life is no longer so simplistic, nor are the roles so clear-cut. Kids today are bombarded by a multitude of choices, then given an eternity to make these choices, without enough guidance.

Ronnie

I wish life were the way it was when my grandfather was little. He talks about the old ways—back when the Indian lived in the bush and there wasn't any alcohol. Now we live on the reservation and life is not the way it was supposed to be. My grandfather never went to school. He would hunt and fish and trade. That is the way life is supposed to be.

I used to go to the pow-wows and learn the old ways. I started to play the drum, but after a while

I began drinking and getting high, too. I disgraced my grandfather by going to a pow-wow high. One time an elder took a feather of mine away. I was ashamed.

I don't want to go back home now. I don't want to go back to school. I don't see why things can't be like they were when my grandfather was little. Back then nobody worried about drinking and getting high. People just did what was right. He would have fun by fishing and dancing and singing—you know, the old way. My friends and I have fun by getting high and stealing. That's not the way it's supposed to be, but that's what we do.

Sometimes I imagine how my life would be if I was born a long time ago or if things were the way they were back then. When I think that way, I don't know where my life is going anymore.

I've done bad in school and now I'm way behind. My family says they don't want me home if I don't get better, if I don't stop getting high. I want to do what is right, but I don't know how. I want to be sober, but all my friends use drugs. I just wish things were the way they were back when my grandfather was my age. I think me and him, we could have been friends.

Peer Pressure and Adolescent Drug Use

During the teenage years, it is normal for kids to pull away from their parents. Their friends become more important than their families. This is a normal and healthy process.

Peer groups offers significant guidance in the young person's search for self. Friendships offer a sense of camaraderie, and drug use has become a common vehicle for a rite of passage. Rules surrounding drug and alcohol use are often dictated by kids. If a child is associating with heavy drug abusers, that child will form rules about drug use based on what the peer group is doing. Getting high then becomes a part of being accepted.

Some people feel that to keep a child drug-free, you mustn't allow him or her to associate with anyone who uses drugs. Unfortunately, it is not that simple. Studies show that most kids will experiment with alcohol and drugs before they graduate from high school. And many kids who wind up in trouble with drugs reported changing peer groups as their drug use increased. As they became more involved with chemicals, their old friends became less important. Instead of following the rules about drug use that were accepted by one set of friends, they found new friends with more acceptable drug use rules.

Karin

I started to drink because some of my friends were drinking. They only drank once in a while and it was cool to just get a buzz. It wasn't too cool to get really drunk. After a few months, I guess we were partying a couple of times a month, on the weekends. But we all still did pretty good in school.

I'm not sure what happened, but it seemed I liked to drink more than my friends. I started to get pretty drunk at some of the parties. My friends laughed at me and it got around school how drunk I had been. I started to get all this attention from other kids who partied more. They were known as being sort of wild and I thought that was exciting. They started to ask me to their parties and I went. I started smoking pot and dropping acid. I really like acid. My old friends heard about that and they thought I was pretty stupid. They didn't want much to do with me after that. In a way it hurt, but in another way I didn't care because I had made these other kids my friends. I really grew away from my old friends. They don't talk to me at all anymore.

Peer pressure plays an important role in teen drug abuse. Kids are strongly influenced by what their friends are doing. The tragic increase in teen suicide among friends (known as suicide pacts) points to just how strong peer bonds can be. However, peer pressure alone is not the cause of the drug problem among young people today.

Early Childhood Trauma and Drug Abuse

I don't believe that any specific trauma causes chemical dependency, but there is some correlation between certain life stressors and adolescent chemical abuse. Some of these stressors include:

- early grief or loss issues
- a history of physical, sexual, or emotional abuse
- neglect
- learning disabilities
- a history of alcohol/chemical abuse in the family

When kids get in trouble with drugs, it is because the chemical use and lifestyle meets many needs—like medicating painful feelings. However, not everyone who experiences a traumatic childhood turns to drug use, and some chemically dependent adolescents had fairly unremarkable childhoods. But, there is a common thread in the lives of children who abuse drugs: they suffer from a poor self-concept. Certain painful events have a negative influence on the formation of a young person's identity.

Grief and Loss

Many kinds of loss have an emotional impact on a young person. The most painful kind of losses involve the death of a loved one or the break-up of a family. However, death and divorce are not the only losses to which kids have a hard time adjusting. Other grief issues that seem to affect adolescents include:

- geographic moves and the loss of friends and neighborhood

- adoption
- the loss of a pet

When the loss happens during childhood, the child will grieve the loss and eventually adjust. However, during the teenage years, the painful feelings and questions often resurface in the young person's search for identity. A common example is adoption. Many young people who know they are adopted seem to adjust well to this fact as children, only to have confusion and uncertainty resurface during adolescence. The identity of their biological parents often becomes very important to them. They want to know what these people look like, what their lives were like, and—most importantly—why they were given up for adoption. Many of the answers they received in the past no longer satisfy them.

It is also common for young people to feel guilty for wanting to know about their biological parents, especially if they feel close to and loved by their adoptive parents. The confusion they experience makes it difficult for them to sort out these emotions, and they can sometimes feel stuck or trapped. I am not suggesting that adoption inevitably leads to chemical abuse. It is, however, one form of grief that some kids experience during adolescence.

Children who have suffered a painful loss often feel as if they are somehow to blame. When a parent dies, it is not uncommon for children to think: *Daddy died because I was mad at him when he sent me to my room and I wished him dead.* Although teens know on an intellectual level that this kind of thinking does not make sense, they sometimes hang on to fragments of these childlike thoughts.

Unresolved grief issues often manifest themselves during the adolescent years through poor bonding skills, a low trust level of others, and a critical sense of self. Chemical use offers these kids easy solutions. Drugs become not only a way to medicate painful and confusing feelings, but also an instant mechanism with which to bond with others.

Kids who have survived traumatic losses also learn at an early age that life can be, and often is, unpredictable and unfair. Grief shatters any illusions of living "happily ever after." These kids learn that relationships don't always last—but they can always count on drugs.

These kids believe that getting high makes them feel good. And when they have alcohol or drugs, they can always find friends.

Other Abuse Issues

Physical, sexual, and emotional abuse are other traumatic life events linked to high-risk kids. Abuse takes a toll on an individual's self-image. Most kids who have been abused feel as if they are to blame. Boys are victimized almost as often as girls, and the perpetrator is usually someone they have known and trusted. One of the most common fears that kids have concerning abuse is that if they tell, they won't be believed.

The most damaging effect of abuse is that it leaves the victim with strong feelings of inadequacy and worthlessness. Victims vacillate between rage and shame and often don't have the verbal or intellectual sophistication to express these intense feelings to others. Because abuse affects self-image so greatly, it is important to understand the kind of coping mechanism chemicals create for abused young people. The chemical not only medicates the painful feelings, but it gives kids a sense of power and confidence in themselves. The euphoria it creates is unequalled. Being high also loosens inhibitions and provides teens with a way to vent their feelings. It is not uncommon for these kids to exhibit promiscuous or volatile behavior while intoxicated. Chemicals give kids permission to act out feelings they have about being abused. Some kids will continue to be victims by becoming involved with people who hurt them. Other kids will become perpetrators by acting out their feelings about being hurt by hurting someone else.

Family History and Chemical Abuse

There is a significant family tendency toward alcoholism and drug abuse. Although there are some new and interesting studies about a possible genetic cause (especially in regard to alcoholism), this information is still too new to be conclusive. In my experience, about 50 percent of the kids in treatment grew up in a home where alcohol or drugs were abused.

Much of what children learn as "normal" behavior is what they see modeled in their homes. Regardless of the verbal messages about chemical use, it is the behavioral messages that make the greatest impact.

Many of the rules about alcohol and chemical use that kids learn are unspoken. If children see a parent making up excuses for another family member's chemically related behaviors, they can learn that chemical use is something you lie about or don't talk about in the house.

Kids can get many other mixed messages when they grow up around alcoholism. As children, they may resent the alcoholic parent and vow to "not turn out that way." However, as kids grow older, these feelings often give way to curiosity as they see their peers experimenting with drugs. Many of these kids don't use alcohol so they won't be like the alcoholic parent. But they often seek out another chemical with which to experiment. Regardless of the drug, kids pattern their use after what they see in the home. If they learn that chemicals are used to relieve stress, they seek stress relief the same way.

Family chemical abuse also affects young people because of the dysfunction it creates in the home. Poor communication skills are marked by dishonesty, blaming, and denial. Children who grow up in a dysfunctional home often believe that they are to blame for the alcoholic's behavior. They sometimes get messages like, "Don't bother Mommy when she's not feeling well," which means, "If Mommy gets upset, it's your fault." The mood swings of an unhealthy parent can cause a young person to feel inadequate.

Jon

Drugs seem like they're the best thing that ever happened to me. Both of my parents are drunks, and when I was little, I said that I would never be like them. Things were pretty scary when I was little. I would hear my folks fighting and some of their fights got bad. I would hide in my room under my bed.

Other things happened, too. We moved a lot, and I never had many friends. I'm not very smart and kids would make fun of me in school. I was really lonely. Sometimes I would come to school with a fat lip and bruises. People would ask me what happened, and I was too ashamed to tell them the truth. I didn't want anyone to know that my old man hit me, so I would make up lies about getting jumped on the way home from school by some bigger kids. All I ever wanted was a place where I fit in.

The last time we moved I decided that things would be different. I heard some kids at the park talking about this great party that they had gone to. I just hung around them and listened for a while. After a few days I got up the nerve to ask them for a joint. At first they laughed at me, but then they got me high. I acted pretty stupid and they laughed, but it all seemed really funny. I liked that a lot. I felt like I fit in with them. Nothing else in the world ever felt so good.

I kept getting high and it always felt good. I don't worry about not fitting in or what my parents are like when I'm high. I don't see why I should quit. Besides, my parents drink, so why shouldn't I use drugs?

Life stressors can damage a young person's self-image, leading to a self-concept that is hurtful and confusing. Other factors that affect self-esteem include:

- learning disabilities
- poor body image
- shyness
- cultural oppression
- spiritual conflict
- poor social skills

Any of these issues can make a young person feel lonely, isolated, and ashamed. It is impossible to shelter kids from painful life events. Sometimes life just hurts. But it is important to recognize the appeal that chemicals have to someone who feels lonely and insecure.

Chemicals offer a sense of comfort and power. Because of this, they offer at least a temporary sense of control. This can be a life-saver to someone who feels like he or she has little or no control.

Chemicals provide kids with an automatic peer group in almost any setting, and they give kids a strong sense of identity. No matter what message kids have heard about the harmful effects of drug use, it only takes one high to realize how great it feels. With all the solutions that chemical use offers, is it any wonder that so many kids are seduced into a lifestyle that involves drug/alcohol use?

Low Self-Esteem and Adolescence

Insecurities are part of the human condition. During the teen years, these feelings are magnified. Struggling with self-esteem is part of life. The most difficult part of that struggle may happen during the teen years. However, some kids are consumed by this struggle. These kids are not just wrestling with the typical adolescent insecurities. These kids, additionally, have a real sense of self-hate. Some of them thrive on trouble, while others are extremely withdrawn and isolated. They are sometimes mislabeled by professionals as antisocial or incorrigible. However, many of these kids are merely acting out a cycle of self-defeating behavior that reflects their poor self-image.

The Cycle of Self-Defeating Behavior

The cycle of self-defeating behavior is a pattern that is present in teens who abuse chemicals. It is a belief system that consists of negative views of themselves and a lack of trust in others. The message they maintain about themselves is "I am not a good person." There tends to be a strong sense of shame. These kids do not see their value and feel isolated and lonely.

The core of their identity is negative self-talk and insecurity. Some of the issues that feed their poor self-image may be traumatic or unresolved events from childhood. They feel hurt, ashamed, lonely, and confused. They hear only negatives and discount their positive qualities. They are highly sensitive to how others perceive them and have difficulty expressing their feelings to others.

Because this is an uncomfortable state for them, they seek out advice and support in an effort to change. They often ask for help out of a sense of desperation. Because they really want to feel better, they make commitments to change. They tell themselves and others that "this time, things will be different." They appear sincere because they are sincere.

For a while, they go through the motions and actually make external changes. But because the new and positive changes do not reflect their internal beliefs, the external changes do not feel comfortable.

When praised, these kids tend to feel anxious. They do not believe that they are good or that they deserve good things. Because the external changes do not reflect their negative self-image, the next phase in the cycle is to create a crisis. The crisis is useful for these kids on several levels. It validates their own sense of self-hate. As crazy as it sounds, this actually makes them feel better. Their external behavior matches their internal belief system. Criticism is more comfortable than praise because it mirrors what they already believe. The crisis behavior also causes the important people in the young person's life to intervene.

They view the attention they receive for acting out as love. As long as the important people in their lives intervene, these kids feel they are loved. This kind of attention feels best because it affirms their internal beliefs. The most comfortable crisis involves chemical use. The drug-induced high medicates the painful feelings that the crisis inevitably produces.

The feelings resulting from each crisis complete the cycle and add a new layer of shame and insecurity. Because these kids do have a conscience and don't like their feelings of self-hate, they start the cycle again, and seek out help or advice. The longer kids are involved in this cycle, the shorter each cycle takes to complete. The self-hate becomes more profound and the cycle more difficult to change. Because adolescents think in concrete terms, they don't have much insight to these kinds of patterns. They simply believe that bad things happen to them because they are bad people.

Nancy

Bob had problems long before he ever began using drugs. His father and I divorced when Bob was seven, and I don't think we handled it well. I hate to admit it, but Bob was a pawn in our separation. We both used him to try to hurt each other. I regret that now.

Bob began to get into trouble shortly after the divorce was final. At first it seemed like the typical acting out and testing that kids do. He'd cause problems in class and the teachers would send notes home. By the time he was ten, things seemed to get more serious. He was caught shoplifting and his grades dropped from Bs and Cs to Ds and Fs. He was beginning to get into fights with other kids in the neighborhood and didn't seem to have any real close friends. Whenever he would get into trouble, he'd feel bad.

At the beginning of each new quarter in school, he'd promise to do better, and for a while he would. But just when it seemed he was going to turn things around, he'd get into trouble again.

By the time Bob was fourteen, I knew he'd been using drugs. He was getting into more and more trouble. He got caught breaking into the neighbor's house; when they pressed charges, he burned down their garage. No one could prove it, but I know Bob did it.

Bob was getting better about being sneaky to avoid consequences, too. But sooner or later, it always seemed to catch up with him. One day, he and some of his friends stole a car and went joy riding. They crashed the car and got arrested. This was the third time he had to go to court. It really shook him up. His probation officer recommended the work squad and set up a strict home contract for him.

Bob did well for about a week. He spent time with me and we had some great talks. He opened up in family counseling for the first time and cried about the divorce. I finally felt like I was getting my son back. I told him how much I loved him and we cried and held each other for a long time. I thought that things were really going to change this time.

The next day, I came home from work and found Bob and a couple of his friends drunk and passed out on the living room floor. They had trashed the house. I don't understand that kid; as soon as we start to get close, he does something to deliberately hurt me.

Living with a child who is entrenched in a cycle of self-defeating behavior can be a living hell. Parents feel like they are on an emotional teeter-totter. They describe countless times when they got their hopes up and believed things would be different. Because they care for the child, they have a hard time seeing the situation objectively.

If you are involved with a young person who behaves in this way, your life will be greatly disrupted. Because these kids do not have any insight into what is going on in their lives, they will often attempt to shift their painful feelings onto those around them by blaming other people or circumstances. It is easy for well-meaning adults to get seduced into this kind of thinking. But this is a trap. It is crucial for these kids to be held accountable for their own behavior.

As a counselor, many times I sat with parents whose faces were lined with worry. They wore the mask of defeat as they told the same story of frustration and fear about losing the child they loved so much. The loss they felt was the loss of control, the loss of dreams, the loss of who they thought their child was. I heard parents describe their bewilderment and anger over not being able to talk with their child anymore. "It's like talking to a brick wall," they said.

They were absolutely right. Somewhere they had lost the ability to communicate with their child. To protect his or her relationship with drugs, the child had built a wall of defenses around his or her drug use.

For the most part, people are good. The vast majority of kids want to do well. They care about other people in their lives. But the abuse of mood-altering substances changes all the rules.

Because chemicals meet so many needs for the addicted adolescent, a strong and unhealthy relationship is developed with the abused substances. It's as if these kids are in love with the drugs and the lifestyle their drugs produce. Kids who are in trouble with drugs never plotted how they were going to protect their relationship with their use. But a pattern of behavior develops out of such a need. I call this pattern of behavior defenses, or "cons."

As the child develops this pattern of defenses, the family counters by developing their own defenses in an attempt to combat the turmoil and craziness they are experiencing. Defenses are useful because they provide us with survival skills in times of crisis. In our society, parents are conditioned to feel responsible for their child's behavior, so when a child exhibits unhealthy behaviors, parents react by adapting themselves to the behaviors their child presents.

Chapter Two

The Brick Wall

Denial

The most prevalent defense—denial—is the first brick in the brick wall. Denial is so common that it is one of the characteristics used to describe chemically dependent people. If a teen admits he or she has a problem with chemicals, then the child is forced to make decisions about whether or not he or she plans to keep using. If the relationship with chemicals meets significant needs, realizing that drugs are a problem may be an insight the child doesn't necessarily want.

When the drug abuser uses denial as a coping mechanism, it creates confusion and conflict in the family. Sincere denial of a chemical problem in the face of an imminent crisis can cause parents to question their own instincts.

Eric

I am so damn sick and tired of my dad bitching about my drinking. He acts like I'm some kind of alcoholic or something. Sure, I get drunk sometimes, but everybody does once in a while. He makes it seem like every single time I drink I get drunk—and that's a crock.

Last night he got all spazzed out because I came home smelling like beer. I had two beers, that's all! Two lousy beers and he acts like I killed somebody. When I told him I only had two beers, he didn't believe me. He's still pissed off because last Saturday night my friends brought me home after I'd had a little too much.

It isn't like I get that drunk every time I drink, it's just that he's been home every time I've gotten drunk. So now he's trying to make a federal case out of two lousy, stinking beers. A lot of my friends drink a hell of a lot more than I do, and their parents don't go crazy. When I tried to tell him that, he said to me, "After what happened on the Fourth of July, you promised not to drink at all anymore."

I don't see how he can still be harping on that. Everyone makes a mistake once in a while, don't they? He keeps throwing it in my face because I got into a stupid accident. A lot of people have accidents when they aren't drinking. Besides, I wasn't even that drunk. It probably would have happened anyway. Nobody was killed, so I don't see what the big stink is about. Just because of one mistake, he expects me not to drink anymore.

Well, that's dumb. All my friends drink. Everybody drinks. I'm just starting my senior year and there is no way in hell that I'm not gonna party this year. Homecoming is next week, and there's Snow Daze and the prom and graduation. This is supposed to be the best year of my life and there is no way that I'm going to go through it like some kind of damn nerd with a pocket protector sipping away at Mountain Dew or Kool Aid or something. It's not like I have a problem or anything. I just like to have a good time. I know when to say when.

Although Eric describes several significant problems related to his drinking, he is adamant that it's not a problem. He justifies his drinking by saying that everybody else does it. He also minimizes the seriousness of an alcohol-related accident by shifting the focus to people who have been in non-alcohol-related accidents.

On the surface, this kind of thinking may be logical. But in reality it just doesn't make sense. By avoiding any responsibility for his drinking behaviors, Eric can continue to deny that his drinking may be a problem. He focuses on a recent incident when he may not have been intoxicated. This is an attempt to avoid any responsibility for the times he was drunk. As long as Eric can deny that his use is a problem, he can continue to give himself permission to drink.

Denial is not used only by the person who has the chemical problem. Family members, especially parents, also go through their own process of denial. For kids in trouble with drugs, denial is a buffer between reality and their love affair with chemicals. For family members, denial is often a mechanism to avoid feeling responsible for the child's out-of-control behaviors. Perhaps the greatest fear that parents have is that somehow they have failed as parents. I know for myself, as a parent, that doing right by my child is perhaps the most important thing I can do in my lifetime. And so much literature out there lays the responsibility for how kids turn out on the heads of the parents. With this kind of conditioning, what parent would want to admit that his or her child has a problem with drugs? On some level that is almost like saying, "I have failed as a parent."

Another significant reason that parents tend to deny that their child has a chemical problem is that they are afraid of losing their dreams about their perfect child. Having a kid who abuses drugs is like having a kid who is somehow broken or defective. Who wants to bring up their child to be an alcoholic or drug addict? The pain of losing a child to drug abuse is magnified by the shame of feeling like a failure as a parent.

Barbara

While my friends were burning their bras and marching on Washington, I was planning a wedding. An old-fashioned wedding, with six brides-maids and the traditional vows that included "to love, honor, and obey," was all I could think about. At that time my life seemed like it was spreading itself out in front of me like a gentle and perfect watercolor. I dreamed of a storybook wedding, which was to be the start of a fairy-tale marriage. Looking back now, I realize that my fantasies were spun out of a troubled and painful childhood, like a web from a small but poisonous spider.

My father spent his time drinking and my mother and I spent our time hiding the fact that Dad drank. We became so good at covering for him and play-acting that ours was a happy home, that I became an accomplished actress before I was twelve. On the outside we had the ideal family. My father was the town sheriff and my mother gave piano lessons and sang solos in the church choir. On the inside we lived a life as predictable and tranquil as trying to skate down the side of a mountain on one roller skate.

I can remember hearing Mom and Dad fight while I was supposed to be asleep. I would put my pillow over my head to soften their screams and crashes and beg God to get me out of their house. I vowed that when I became a mother my children would have happy parents who loved each other and smiled all the time.

I was eighteen when I married Bill. He was my Knight in Shining Armor, and I was sure he was going to take me away from the darkness of my parents' home and bring light to my life like stars to the night. We both wanted children and tried for a long time to have a baby. Nine years later, we were still without children. I began the business of grieving my dreams of being a mother. I realized I would have to accept the fact that we would be childless.

It was during this time I found out I was pregnant. What a surprise! What a joy! I thanked God for this miracle and vowed to Him that my child would never know the pain and disappointment I had wrestled with as a child. I loved Eric from the very second I found out that I was pregnant. I could feel Eric grow inside of me, and when he was still I would find myself kneading my belly, like a large pan of dough, in an attempt to feel his life kick back at me. Before he was born I would read him stories and play him classical music. My joy grew in proportion to my girth.

After he was born, I was transformed. Eric was my love, my life, and my world. I reveled in his firsts— his first step, first word, first day of school, first bicycle, first Little League game, and first love.

But the first time Eric came home drunk—that was a first I wasn't prepared for. He was only thirteen. I tried to tell myself that it was just a phase. That all kids try drinking once or twice. I didn't tell Bill about it because I thought that he'd be mad. Now I don't know what to think.

I've seen Eric drunk so many times that I can't even count them all. Bill says that our boy has a problem, but I just don't know. Sure, last summer when he had the accident, he was really scared. He totalled the car and he didn't even have a license. Thank God he wasn't hurt badly, only bumped up a little. Bill really lost it when that happened, and I guess Eric was pretty scared, too. He promised us that he'd never drink again and I was relieved. But you know how kids are. Drinking is really just a part of growing up, isn't it? Besides, we've been good parents—at least, I think we have. So how can Eric have a problem with alcohol? It's not like he drinks every day. If he did that, I'd know he has a problem. Dad drank every day—well, at the end he did. And Eric's not like him! He can't be.

Sometimes, though, I think there is something wrong. We aren't close like we used to be. And there's all this anger. It's like all the love we used to have has evaporated in the steam of all the hostility that boils in the house. Maybe he's going through another phase. I know kids are supposed to be moody. Maybe Bill expects too much from him and that makes him moody. Every time the poor kid comes home with red eyes, Bill automatically assumes that he has been drinking. I think it's allergies. Sometimes when Bill accuses Eric of smelling like alcohol, Eric swears it's Dentyne gum. It smells like gum to me, and besides, Eric is a good kid. He wouldn't lie about something like that. There have been plenty of times when he's come home drunk and told us that he'd been drinking. I just can't believe it's gotten as bad as Bill says it has. I do wish Eric wouldn't drink at all. I get scared that if he isn't careful, he'll wind up like Daddy and really have an alcohol problem. I couldn't stand it if that happened. I'd feel like somehow it was my fault.

Eric says it's not an alcohol problem. He admits that he's having some troubles right now, but he thinks they're emotional or something. Maybe he's right. He's always been a sensitive child, and he's always had a temper. So maybe it has nothing to do with his drinking. I've seen kids in our neighborhood go through treatment, and they come back and nothing changes. In fact, Eric hangs out with some of those kids now.

I've talked to Eric about my concerns, but he makes me feel so foolish. When he talks he's so convincing. He tells me everything is okay. If he's that sure he doesn't have a problem, then maybe I don't have anything to worry about.

Parental love is not always enough to stop a kid from getting in trouble with drugs. Once the problem has started to develop, it is futile to try and sweep it away. Most parents want to believe their children, and sometimes it's easy to believe the lies because it's too painful to believe the truth. For many parents, doubting their kids is the same as doubting themselves. Other parents listen to the stories of denial that their kids tell and feel trapped and confused.

Bill

I'm not sure when everything started to fall apart, but it sure came tumbling down around us like a building being demolished by a wrecking ball. Barb has always had a blind spot where the kid is concerned, and sometimes I think that's okay, because everyone needs someone on their side. Besides, I've been busy with work and I know I can be hard to live with because I expect so much. This last year has been a living hell, though. Eric will come home smelling like a cheap tavern and try and tell us he's been chewing gum. We'll get into it and then Barbie will say that it smells like gum to her. Maybe she's right. I've seen the kid drunk so many times that maybe I'm looking for things that aren't there. There have been times when I was certain he was lying to us about where he'd been. I'd be sure that he'd been out with those good-for-nothings who he parties with and he'd swear on the Pope's grave that he was at a game, or something like that. We'd go around and around and after a while I'd start to feel crazy, like maybe the kid's telling the truth and I'm nothing but an unreasonable old ogre. Barb never doubts him, and I have to admit that a lot of the time when I confront Eric, it's Barb and I who wind up fighting (she always takes his side). I used to trust my instincts, but I just don't know anymore. The whole thing makes me pretty damned tired.

◆◆◆

Because we want to hear the truth from our children, denial and lies can throw us off and make us feel crazy. It is hard to believe that when your kid is lying to you about using chemicals, he or she is choosing drugs over relationships—the child is choosing drugs over you. Although this is not a conscious choice, the pain of it can be felt on some deep level by both the child and the people who love that child.

Blame

Another defense that constructs the brick wall is blame. Usually blame will surface after the problem has been clearly pointed out and denial no longer works. The prime purpose of blame is to shift the focus from the person with the drug problem to someone or something else, so that the relationship with the drug use is protected. Because one of the roles of a "good parent" is to protect the child from harm or from the unfairness of the world, this defense works well in the parent/child relationship.

Rita

When Suzanne came home from a date three hours later than her curfew, I was upset. I was worried. No, I was scared. She's the oldest, and I know I depend on her a lot with her younger brother and sister, but she's still my baby, too. I didn't mean to sound angry, but that's how I come across when I'm scared.

"Where have you been?" I snapped.

"Out."

"That's not good enough, young lady! I told you to be home by 11:00. Tomorrow is a school day," I said. I could feel my insides tighten up. It was as if a tornado was twisting around inside of me.

"Don't start with me, Mother," Suzanne shrieked at me. I could see that her eyes were glassy and red.

"You've been getting high!" I whispered hoarsely. I was beginning to worry that we'd wake the little ones.

"So what," she snapped. "It's not like you've never gotten high, Mother!"

"That's not fair, Suzanne."

"No, Mother! You know what's not fair? It's not fair that I had to grow up without a father. It's not fair that you spent my whole childhood smoking up a storm and running around. I had to take care of you and now you want to spoil my fun. You're the one with a drug problem, Mother, remember?"

That's how the fights always seem to go. When I try to hold Suzanne accountable, she brings up the fact that I wasn't a very good mother when she was little—and she's right. I feel so guilty. I've been recovering for fourteen months now, but I wasn't there for her when she was little. I wasn't there for her when it counted.

◆◆◆

Suzanne's mother describes how effective blame can be. As parents, we are conditioned to stick up for our kids. We all know how it feels to have our children come home in tears because of the bully down the street, or because they have a teacher who doesn't like them. Because we are conditioned to be our children's protectors, we often try to blame their problems on someone else. Kids seem to instinctively know this. Kids also seem to know just what weaknesses their parents will feel guilty about. I know that as a teenager, I did. Now, after having the experience of parenting teens, I have first-hand knowledge of how awful it feels to be on the other side of that blame. Blaming your parents at just the right time can get you out of some pretty tight spots. Feeling guilty about not being a "good parent" is one of the worst feelings I know. Other ways we can get sucked into blame as a defense is to not hold our kids accountable because of other injustices they have suffered.

Bonnie

Josh is really a good kid. It's just that he's always had these problems that make him different. He's hyperactive and he has dyslexia. I can remember when he was just a little guy, and he'd come home from school crying because of something that had happened in school.

"I'm just a dummy," he would say. He wouldn't want to tell me what had happened. But after a

while it would always come out that he had been fidgeting and that he'd made the class laugh, or that he had gotten confused and read something wrong and the other kids would laugh at that, too. Then the teacher would be upset with him. You don't know how many times I had to go down to that school to fight with those teachers. By the time he was in third grade, he'd already developed a reputation as class clown and troublemaker. No one understood what a sensitive kid Josh really was. Now his school is calling me and telling me that he is getting high. They say that he was caught selling drugs in school and they want me to do something about it. It really gets me, after all the times I went down there because of his learning disabilities. I begged them to help Josh, and I always got the same answer: "Mrs. Jackson, there is only so much we can do."

Well, now I feel like there's only so much that I can do. Maybe they should have done more when he was smaller. Maybe if they had, he wouldn't have the problem now.

Many of us look at our children's lives and understand why they would abuse drugs. We have felt the pain and injustice of their lives, and we have even tried to fight some of their battles for them. This can become a danger-ous game when drugs are involved. By allow-ing ourselves to accept the pain in our kid's lives as a justification for their behavior, we can inadvertently give them permission to continue using chemicals and also continue on their self-destructive march. I am not suggesting that we close our hearts to the troubles our kids have been facing, but excusing their behavior because of their troubles gives kids permission to continue their drug use.

Anger

Anger is perhaps the most powerful and frightening defense that chemical abuse produces. Families who have experienced their child's rage are often caught in a whirl of changing values, dreams, and hopes. Because having your child exhibit hate is so contrary to the picture of a family, families who have experienced this are often filled with shame, fear, and feelings of inadequacy. The conflict that this kind of anger creates in the home leaves no family member unaffected. Although anger is a normal emotion, there are healthy ways to express anger and not-so-healthy ways to express anger. The less healthy ways range from sulking or cold silence to explosive fits of anger. Anger used as a defense is more like a strategy in a war game than an emotion. "If you threaten to take what is valuable from me, I just might attack you. My drug use is important to me—don't try to stop my partying."

Marge

I never thought I would see the day when I would be afraid of one of my kids. Rick has a temper and the kids have seen us fight more than once, but I never thought that one of my kids would be this out of control. Scott is big for his age, and he's always been strong-willed. But this last year things have gotten completely out of hand.

When Rick's not around and I try to set a limit with Scott, he usually ignores me. When I try to be more forceful, he'll give me a look like he would like to kill me. At first I would stand up to him and we would argue. Some of the names he would call me make me sick. He has called me a "bitch," a "fat slob," and a "whore." It tears me apart to think about it.

Scott has broken doors and threatened me with his fists. Sometimes when Rick is home they actually come to blows. I never felt like I could tell anyone that. We don't talk about this with anybody. I don't think anybody else would understand. Sometimes I worry about the effect it has on Gina. She's only eight and she's lived with this escalating rage for more than two years now. Maybe she doesn't know what's really going on. I've told her Scott has a drug problem. I'm not even sure she knows what that means—she's still so young, and besides, she doesn't ever seem to be around when things get out of hand.

This sounds terrible, but there have been times when Scott has left the house in a rage and I wished he just wouldn't come back. Then I hated myself for thinking that, because I'm afraid he might overdose or get killed or something. I don't know if I could live with myself if that happened. I just pray that this doesn't affect Gina too much.

Gina

Scott makes me cry sometimes, but I don't let him see me cry, because that will make it worse. I used to want to be around him, but now I don't. Sometimes he calls me a baby or a pussy when he sees me cry. Then he hits me in the head. I know a lot about what he does that Mom and Dad don't know, but I'm not gonna tell. Scott gets high in his room a lot. I see him smoke that stuff all the time. I told on him once and later Scott tore the head off my doll and spit at me. When I started to cry, he hit me in the head. At Christmas time things got really bad. Scott was doing something that made Mom and Dad mad. I think he wasn't coming home or something. They all started yelling and stuff. Dad said some bad things to Scott, then Scott said some bad things back. Dad's face got all red and I thought he was going to die. I started to cry. Scott put his fist through the wall and said more bad things and then he left the house. I was glad that he left. When I went to see Santa Claus at the mall, I asked for Santa to make Scott dead. He said he thought that I really wanted something else. I said "No, I want Scott dead." Sometimes when things get really bad, I hide under my bed. No one can hurt me if I'm under my bed. Sometimes I fall asleep there. Mom says that Scott has a drug problem. I hate drugs. I'm never gonna do drugs. I hate Scott.

◆◆◆

Anger and rage can be powerful deterrents for parents in their attempt to confront a drug problem. The kind of rage Marge and Gina describe in Scott is not unusual with adolescents who have completely invested themselves in a drug-oriented lifestyle. The greater the investment, the greater the fight when the relationship with the drug is threatened. Fits of rage or violence, running away from home, and long, angry silences are all signs of anger used as a defense.

Outbursts of rage fit neatly into the crisis phase of the cycle of self-defeating behaviors. Most kids who exhibit these kinds of behaviors hate themselves for doing so, and then wind up medicating their feelings with drugs. At that time, their denial conveniently kicks in and they often blame the person with whom they had their conflict. However, in treatment, when these kids reexamine their behaviors, they become painfully in touch with their own self-hate. Then they are faced with the brutal fact that they have injured the people they love the most because they have chosen drugs over their families. This is especially true when they have used verbal or physical violence to protect their relationship with drugs.

The Sibling Factor

In the previous section, Gina's story describes how a sibling can be affected by chemical use in the family. Her feelings of fear and dislike are not uncommon. It is typical for younger siblings to look up to their older brothers and sisters. Little kids want to be like big kids. Often siblings will know more about what is going on with their brother or sister than parents will. In Gina's case, fear stopped her from telling her parents about her brother's drug use and related behaviors. Many times, a strong need to be liked will keep a sibling quiet. What kid wants to be known in the family as a snitch or tattletale or narc? It is often more important for kids to work for acceptance from their siblings than from their parents. Sometimes this need for acceptance can lure the siblings into experimenting with chemical use of their own.

Terry

When I was nine, my brother Jon was fifteen. I used to think he was so cool. I wanted to be just like him. I would be really boosted if he would let me come along with him and his friends. It made me feel grown-up or something. Most of the time he treated me like a dork, so when he included me, I was careful to try and be what he wanted me to be. I knew he would go out and party with his friends when Mom and Dad thought he was just spending the night at a friend's house. Sometimes he would even tell me how blasted he had gotten. I thought he was so cool. It made me really curious about alcohol. I also felt kind of important because he was trusting me with a secret that he would never tell Mom or Dad. No way was I going to betray that trust. Right after my tenth birthday, Mom and Dad had to go out of town because my grandpa got real sick and had to go into the nursing home. They left Jon and me at home. Jon was supposed to babysit me, but he had a party instead. He invited about twenty kids from high school. At first I was scared. I knew our parents wouldn't like it, and everyone was so loud that I was afraid that we'd get into trouble. I was kind of hanging back until some girl fell over and broke a glass window on Mom's china hutch. I went to Jon and told him that I didn't think the party was a good idea. I was almost crying because I didn't know what we were going to do about the broken hutch. I remember, Jon was already pretty drunk. He messed up my hair and said, "Don't worry, little man. Here, have a beer." I didn't know what to do, then his girlfriend started talking about how cute I was. That night was the first time I ever drank. The thing I remember most about that whole night is that I felt like I went from being the pesty little brother to "one of the guys" with just one glass of beer.

Siblings can have a wide and varied response to a brother or sister's use. They can be fearful and angry or they may look up to, even idolize, the chemical abuser. Many kids may not understand everything that is going on, but they know they don't like conflict or fighting. Sometimes these kids wind up trying to be the "peacemakers" in the family by keeping secrets or covering up for the chemical abuser. Siblings seem to have a great deal of knowledge about their brother or sister's drug use. They also seem to have a treasure trove of reasons for keeping this information hidden from adults in their lives. Understanding how the other children are affected may not be as important as just recognizing that they have been affected in the first place.

The Family Behind the Brick Wall

The brick wall that I have described isn't built overnight. It happens over a period of time. As children's dependence on drugs grow, they become more protective of their relationship with drugs. As this happens, they exhibit more defensiveness about their behaviors. Denial is the first defense. Because families tend to believe their children, they are often easily seduced into accepting the denial. While kids tend to minimize their drug use, parents do their own minimizing with statements like "If it's only alcohol, I don't need to worry," and "All kids experiment—it's only a phase."

As the denial continues to grow, kids will justify their behaviors, and many times parents find themselves justifying as well, with statements like "It's okay if she uses as long as I know about it. You can't expect kids not to use at Homecoming. I know that I did."

Justification leads to blaming. Once we begin to believe there are valid reasons for our kids to use mood-altering substances, it is easy to believe that there are other sources on which to blame their drug abuse. By making this shift in thinking (although we may not mean to), we, in fact, give the young person a reason to continue using drugs.

"I'm not surprised that Jess uses. After all, my husband is an alcoholic, and that's the major role model that Jess has grown up with," or, "I can't blame Carrie for how she is. I've been a single parent and we've moved a lot. She's had a hard life and I haven't always been there for her. What right do I have in trying to tell her how to live?" On one level these justifications may make sense, but they also excuse the young person from taking the responsibility for change.

Chapter Three

When the Drug War Hits Home

If you think that your child has a problem with chemicals, if you are uncomfortable with the relationship that your child is establishing with chemicals, or if the limits you have set aren't working, then it's probably time to seek professional help. This can be a scary process because it means that you are admitting that what you have tried doesn't work, and that you need to try something else. It also means that you might wind up trusting a complete stranger to care for your child.

Many agencies offer assessments to determine if treatment is necessary and, if so, what level of care is needed. Some places even offer free assessments. If you don't know where to go, you can start by checking with your local school, social service agencies, church or synagogue, community center, counseling agencies, hospital, emergency hotlines, or A.A. group. One of these agencies can direct you to someone who has experience with adolescent assessments.

Be prepared to bring as much concrete data as you can to the assessment. You may find it useful to talk with the people at your child's school or with others who may have information about your child's drug use and related behaviors.

Assessments usually take from one to three hours. You and your child will be interviewed during this time. Some agencies do these interviews separately, while others do them "intervention style." That is, after the data is gathered by concerned persons, the child is confronted with the information that was collected. At the end of the assessment, a determination is usually made as to whether or not the adolescent needs treatment and, if so, what kind.

The least restrictive method of treatment should be recommended. When choosing the level of care, some important factors need to be considered, such as if the child is at risk to hurt him or herself or others. The best way to deal with this is to tackle the problem without removing the child from the home or school setting. If the child is still doing fairly well in school and shows satisfactory impulse control, as well as the ability to follow through with directives, a "no chemical use" contract in conjunction with outpatient (individual or family) counseling can be recommended.

There are other levels of care. One is a highly structured outpatient program. This program usually meets three to five times a week, includes family involvement, and may interrupt some or all of the school day, but the patient remains at home. Another possibility is the inpatient program, which means that the adolescent is placed in a residential program either in a hospital or an independent agency. These programs can have open units or secured units that are equipped to handle kids requiring a higher level of care.

Follow-up studies show that kids who receive early intervention tend to do better than their peers who are not confronted until their use and lifestyles are out of control. Once kids have reached the point where they are running away, experiencing multiple arrests or bouts of violence and self-destructive behaviors, or attempting prostitution or suicide, they have a more difficult time maintaining progress in their recovery. However, the trend in our country right now has moved away from early intervention. Many third-party reimbursers (i.e., medical insurers and managed care providers) will not recognize the chemical problem when a less restrictive mode of treatment will be most effective. As a result, many people cannot access treatment for their kids until the problem has deteriorated to the point where it is life-threatening. The irony is that these same reimbursers will then deny treatment for these same kids because they do not show the proper motivation for treatment.

From an economic standpoint, I can understand the need to have certain constraints to hold down the cost of health care, but as a mother and a human being with compassion, I know that a lot of kids and families wind up falling between the cracks because they cannot access the level of care they need when they need it. To make early intervention more difficult, our culture seems bent on criminalizing chemical abuse. As a nation, we want to minimize how widespread adolescent drug use is. We seem to want to solve this problem politically by having tougher laws. I fail to understand what mandatory sentences for drug abusers will accomplish. Surely we do not believe that the guy on the corner with a rock of crack in his pocket is responsible for the epidemic that seems to have stricken our youth. Although I advocate holding the abuser accountable for all of his or her behaviors, I believe we are being both hysterical and foolish to think that throwing the alcohol or drug abuser in jail will deter the growing chemical problem. As a nation, we need to ask ourselves two important questions:

1. What is lacking in young people's lives that makes chemical use so appealing?

2. What can we do to convince our communities and health care providers that

early intervention and treatment has a higher success rate than waiting until the young person is completely invested in a chemically-oriented lifestyle?

It's like the old adage, "A stitch in time saves nine." We need to address this problem before it is life-threatening, before the child or the family has been irrevocably damaged, and before the community has to pay the larger price for an escalating drug problem.

Shopping for a Treatment Setting

You probably wouldn't buy the first car you see, so it makes sense to shop around for a treatment program. However, based on where you live and how the treatment is going to be paid for, you may not have a lot of options. Talk with other families who have had a son or daughter in treatment and explore what their experience has been. Just as there are different makes of cars, there are different models for treatment. Programs that are designed for adolescents are the best. Adult models simply do not serve the younger population well. Kids tend to be at a much different place cognitively, emotionally, and socially.

I also feel strongly that Alcoholics Anonymous (A.A.) programs offer a more practical approach than some other models. The twelve-step philosophy of A.A. addresses chemical dependency on a spiritual level. Let us not confuse spirituality with religion. Religion is the organized study and practice of faith. Spirituality is the internal connection we feel with God, our universe, other people, and living things, as well as a consciousness that we are a part of something much larger. Spirituality is the element that makes us care about who we are and how our behaviors affect those whose lives we touch. Twelve-step programs seem to address these issues on a universal level. These steps can coincide with virtually any religious sect or with people who might be described as agnostic, or without a structured religious belief.

I also believe that A.A.-based treatment settings are preferable because part of the rehabilitation process helps kids redefine who they are. Since twelve-step groups are probably the most common support groups out there, kids who have been in one of these programs are provided with an automatic peer group and support system when they leave the treatment setting. Remember, one of the most powerful things a chemically-centered lifestyle does for kids is provide them with instant friends. It is important to provide an atmosphere to meet some different kids who will support your child's abstinence.

Lastly, the A.A. philosophy not only helps us understand ourselves better, it provides us with new tools to make lasting changes in our lives. Let's face it, all the insight in the world won't do much good if you don't know how to change.

When searching for a treatment facility, find a program that won't kick kids out for the same kinds of behaviors that got them in there. We must expect that a lot of these kids are going to have a rocky path ahead of them. If your child exhibits self-defeating behavior, you might want to investigate how the program will handle it if he or she violates major rules (such as getting high, fighting, or breaking sexual contact rules). Look for a program that has experience with holding kids accountable without kicking them out. Lastly, and most importantly, find a program that has a family component, as well as a well-developed community support network. Since everybody is affected in some way by a young person's chemical abuse, it is important that siblings—as well as parents—receive professional help.

Unfortunately, in these times, you may not be given the freedom to "shop" for a program that fits the needs of you and your child. Insurance companies, public policies, and financial reviewers are making these decisions based on the dollar instead of the appropriate level of care.

We're in Treatment . . . Now What?

Entering your child in a treatment program may leave you feeling scared and helpless or incredibly relieved. Be prepared, though, because the days ahead will bring a roller coaster of emotions.

If your child is in an outpatient program, you will also be challenged. As he or she experiences the highs and lows of the next several weeks, you will be right there, observing. You must maintain your perspective, seek support, and allow your child to struggle—your struggle will be to "share" the emotional volatility of your child's work without losing yourself in it.

As kids and families get used to a way of life that excludes mood-altering substances and includes a new set of rules, they go through a metamorphosis of internal change. Going through this change together forces a change in communication. Because the nature of change can be so intense, however, it can create conflict—more than some families and kids can handle. Therefore, it is essential that families continue to seek appropriate support.

If your child is in an inpatient setting, you will be faced with a different set of adjustments to make while he or she is gone. Some families find that for the first time in a long time, they have peace and quiet in their home. This can be either a source of relief and comfort, or it can cause parents to feel guilty—because they feel relieved and comforted that their kid isn't around.

Sometimes the guilty feelings can give way to old defenses, such as self-blame and denial. In the initial phase of treatment, kids quickly get in touch with the fact that they are no longer in control. They may be homesick or scared. The fear is usually related to the kinds of changes they will be expected to make. Because they have relied so heavily on chemicals to feel good, they often feel stripped and alone when they no longer have the option to use. Since they are no longer medicating painful feelings, all the emotions they haven't felt while using come crashing in on them. During this initial phase in treatment, kids often look depressed and sound desperate. They deny that their use is a problem and they often start to exhibit the same defenses that they used with their families to avoid responsibility for change. The combination of families who are feeling guilty and kids who are feeling desperate results in another form of "splitting."

Bud

When I first dropped Kathy off at rehab, I felt incredible relief. She had been on the run for two weeks and we didn't know if she was dead or alive. Before she ran away, our lives were a nightmare. She had stolen so much money and jewelry from us that I had to put a lock on our bedroom door and my wife, Kate, would have to hide her purse and car keys. When Kathy wasn't out getting high, she was either sulking in her room or fighting with one of us. We have holes in the walls that are the signature of her rage. I don't know how many times she tormented her little brother. Danny was so afraid of her that sometimes he would start to cry if she just walked into the room.

The worst night of my life was when I came home to find Kathy high and threatening Kate with a knife. I tried to restrain her and she swung the knife toward me. I slapped the knife away and I hit her. I've never hit one of my kids. I gave my daughter a black eye.

When we dropped her off for treatment I felt peaceful for the first time in years. But, on the way home on the plane I began to feel a little sad that I had to leave my little girl almost 2,000 miles away. The next few days were really peaceful, but they were also hard, because all I could think of was, where did we go wrong?

Then the phone call came from Kathy. She was hysterical. She begged us to get her out of there. She said the counselors were mean, that they didn't understand her, and she said the other kids were a bunch of criminals.

Something inside me snapped. I forgot all the crap that we had been going through the past four years. I forgot about having to lock the doors, I forgot about the fear in Danny's eyes, I forgot about the time that Kathy had tried to stab my wife, and the sleepless nights when she was on the run doing God knows what. They just vanished from my mind. All I could think of was that my little girl was upset and that she needed me and that she was 2,000 miles away with counselors who didn't understand her and a bunch of juvenile delinquents. You know, I almost got on a plane that night to get her. When Kate got home I told her about the call. She had the wisdom to suggest that we call the staff at the center and talk with them first. After talking with the staff, I felt better. We left Kathy there, but it was hard.

◆◆◆

When you leave a child in the hands of someone else it usually is because you have come to
a point in your life where you have exhausted
all your own resources. This can be a time of
pain and uncertainty. Many families report
feeling helpless and hopeless. It is at this time
that families really need to come together for
support, comfort, and guidance. This kind of
help can be found in any twelve-step group
designed for family members. Groups like
Families Anonymous, Tough Love, and Al-
anon have different personalities. It is important to shop around to find the one that meets
your needs.

The Treatment Process

The treatment process is just that, a process.
It has a beginning, a middle, and an end. It is
filled with peaks and valleys. For kids who are
accustomed to creating crises in their lives, for
kids who are filled with self-doubt and self-
hate, for kids who are entrenched in a chemically-oriented lifestyle, this period of time is
chaotic at best. One day you may get a positive
progress report on your child and the next you
may find out that this same kid has either run
away or has violated an important rule. This
can be a source of frustration and confusion
for families. The most often asked question
is, "How could this happen? Just yesterday we
had such glowing reports!" The answer usually
involves the fact that these kids are still caught
in their cycle of self-defeating behavior, which

they have very little control over. However, an experienced treatment staff should be able to work with these kids to help them turn these crises into learning experiences.

Even with professional help, many kids find this pattern extremely difficult to change. They seem to make progress, only to sabotage it all at the very end.

As much as we would like to believe that treatment offers magic, we need to understand that it is only a beginning. Treatment is the very beginning of a recovery process for kids, a process that is often slow and painful. Just going through adolescence is challenging. To go through it as a young person with a chemical abuse problem can be a monumental task.

The bulk of the adolescent's treatment may focus on coming to terms with the fact that his or her drug use is both harmful and out of control, and at the same time, the child is terrified of life without drugs or alcohol. Because the chemically-oriented lifestyle meets so many social and emotional needs for kids, this is a struggle that they wrestle with for weeks and even months after they have completed treatment. A.A. describes this phase of recovery as the first step.

Step 1: We admitted we were powerless over alcohol–that our lives had become unmanageable.

The first step for kids involves facing their love affair with a self-destructive lifestyle. If you are familiar with the story of Dr. Doolittle, you may remember the "Push-me-pull-you." This was the mythical animal that was constantly wanting to go in two directions at once. That is how a first step feels for kids. In this step, kids begin to get in touch with the fact that their use has hurt them, hurt the people they love, and generally messed up their lives. But they are also painfully aware of the fact that their use and using lifestyle has brought them friends, comfort, and a sense of personal reputation and pride. They feel torn between wanting to give up their chemicals and wanting nothing more than to get high—NOW. Kids see life in absolutes, in black and white. They have a hard time accepting that these two conflicting emotions and desires can and do exist at the same time. During this point in treatment, kids are not able to, and should not be expected to, make a commitment to recovery. Working through this step can take longer than the other steps, because this is where the brick wall of defenses is addressed.

Kathy

I know that my use is a problem. I guess I've known it for about a year now. At first it was fun. Sure, I had a few consequences—like a hangover or cotton mouth or doing something stupid at a party—but nothing really bad happened for so long that I really thought I could keep it under control. I can't.

My God! I tried to kill my mother, and I don't even remember it! I guess I was going to stab her and then my dad stopped me. There have been plenty of times that I have threatened to kill her. I would say, "You'd better lock your door tonight if you want to wake up tomorrow."

I really hated my parents. I hated them because they were getting in the way. It felt like they were trying to control me. They would ask me questions about what I was up to—there was no way I was going to tell them. Sometimes I would get into a fight with them just to have an excuse to get out of the house and get high. I wished they were dead so that they wouldn't get in my way. Sometimes I would be gone for days or weeks. I would stay so loaded that nothing else seemed to matter. My parents would die if they knew some of the things I did just to survive out there. Hell, they'd really die if they knew what I did just to get my drugs.

I think about all of this stuff, and it scares me—it makes me sick. I hate myself, but I still want to get high. My counselor asked me how I felt about this stuff and I said that I felt lousy. I said that I was ashamed because I really do love my parents. Then he asked me, "If you could get high in your room tonight and not get caught, would you do it?" I thought about it for a while, because I really do want to get better and I know I have to start being honest. I couldn't get away from it. If I could get high right now, I'd do it. I want to feel good again, and getting high makes me feel good. So I said, "Yeah, I'd do it. I'd get high right now if I could." Then this one kid in my group said, "Your drugs are still more important than your family. You'd pick getting high over your parents because you love it more." I said "screw you" to him. Then he tried to tell me that he understood that because he was the same way. I hate it here and I hate these people. I just want to get away.

The First Step for Families

While kids are struggling with their own feelings of powerlessness and unmanageability, parents and family members are faced with a similar emotional conflict. The powerlessness that families are faced with is related to the fact that they could not prevent the dependency, nor could they control their child's behavior while they were involved with drugs. Many families must also admit to being out of control, even before their child began getting high. Parents often feel they are to blame—that they have failed as parents. Unmanageability for parents can also come in the form of the lengths that parents will, and often do, go to in an attempt to control their child's behavior.

Much of what is written for family members on these issues (often referred to as co-dependency) is directed toward adult relationships. There may be some value in this information on the importance of letting go, but these rules don't apply in the same way when we are talking about your relationship with your child. The irony is, even though you cannot control your child's behavior, you still may find yourself legally responsible for what the child does and how he or she does it. This can create incredible feelings of helplessness and frustration.

First step issues for parents include trying to separate feelings about who your child is from feelings about what your child does. This can be hard to do. It may have been a long time since you have seen your child without the influence of chemicals. Parents sometimes get caught trying to understand the reasons that their child is on drugs. This can sidetrack them from the issue at hand, as well as from focusing on how they have been affected by their child's substance abuse problem. To make this even more complicated, parents also find themselves in the position of having to try to come out of this uncontrollable craziness with a sense of being in charge.

Kate

Bud and I have been through the mill the past few years. At first, when we realized that Kathy had a problem, we tried to minimize it to ourselves and to the rest of our family. My parents are hyper-critical of Bud and me and how we raise the kids. They can be very judgmental, but I love them and I am close to them. We have really worked hard to hide from them what has been going on. Right now they think Kathy is away at summer camp. They don't have any idea that she's in a drug rehabilitation program. They're very "old world" and it would kill them.

Two years ago, when Bud and I started to get concerned, we had a lot of discussions on what to do. I talked to our priest and Bud almost went through the ceiling. He said that it is our problem and we should solve it by ourselves. We fought about it a lot. But then, when she started to steal from us, Bud agreed that we had to do something. We took Kathy to see a psychologist. Bud said that a guy he knew from work had the same kind of problems with his son. They started to see this doctor and then everything seemed to straighten out. Well, we went to see this man and do you know what he told us? He told us that we were being too strict, and that Kathy was rebelling against our control. He said that she was feeling pressured by us and that our expectations of her were too high. He said that this was causing her to have some kind of an "adjustment reaction." That's what he called it, an "adjustment reaction!" Then he told us to "lighten up." He said that we should "loosen our control and give her some more freedom."

Bud and I went home feeling guiltier then ever. We felt that we were the cause of our daughter's problems. But we did as we were told. We "loosened up" and gave her freedom. That's when things really got nuts.

The next six months Bud and I fought more than ever. We took turns blaming each other for what she was doing. Believe me, she was doing it with a vengeance! Then she started to run away, and we all went berserk. It was then that we realized that maybe, just maybe, Kathy had conned the psychologist, so we decided to clamp down.

You wouldn't believe the things we did to try and control Kathy. Once Bud tackled her on her way out of the house and then carried her to her room and locked her in. But he forgot to lock the windows. She climbed out, shimmied down the tree, then went out to a party. He's had the phone tapped and even hired a private investigator to bring her back once when she ran away. The whole time this was going on we managed to hide everything from our family and most of our friends.

I was pretty busy, too. I heard someone talk about the chemical imbalance in chemically dependent people, so I tried to get Kathy to take a lot of vitamins. I would go back and forth between trying to bribe her to be "good" with money and clothes and threaten her when she was "bad" with taking those things away. It never occurred to me that she really didn't care what I did as long as she could get out and get high.

The craziest I got was when she came back from being gone for three days. While she was sleeping it off I stayed up all night and sewed all her clothes shut at the openings. I sewed her sleeves shut and her pant legs shut! I thought that if all she had was a nightgown she wouldn't be able to go anywhere. You can probably imagine how well that worked. She stayed home a few days and made our lives miserable, then she went into my room and took some jeans and a sweater and left.

During all of this (and even now), I didn't know whether to love her or hate her. I feel love and hate for Bud and myself, too. I feel a lot of guilt because we have always put a lot of pressure on the kids and we haven't always been there for them. Maybe if we had been better parents when Kathy was little, she wouldn't have needed to get high. Then I start to think of all the things that I should do to make her well. But some of my ideas aren't much better than sewing her clothes shut. Sometimes I just give up—I just want to run away from home myself.

By internalizing the first step, both kids and their families get in touch with just how out of control their lives have become because of chemical abuse. They also gain the awareness that even though their lives were no longer manageable, they still fought to maintain some kind of control—which in many instances, made the situation worse rather than better. Although some of this can be very painful to see, we can learn to laugh at some of the things that we did in desperation. With the laughter, healing will begin.

Other people who have experienced the same fears and frustrations may be able to help us in gaining some of this objectivity. These people can be found in twelve-step groups for parents (i.e., Families Anonymous and Tough Love groups). Part of healing is knowing and paying attention to the pain, the shame, the guilt, and the sadness. But another part of healing is being able to laugh at our humanness and move on.

Chapter Four

The Healing Begins

Step 2: Came to believe that a power greater than ourselves could restore us to sanity.

Step 3: Made a decision to turn our will and our lives over to the care of God as we understood Him.

These steps for adolescents involve trusting, risking, and placing needs before wants. This can be difficult for young people who have experienced trauma because these events can leave kids with limited trusting and bonding abilities. Even if they are able to bridge this gap, they may not feel worthy of the care offered to them. Whether the treatment program goes through the steps of A.A. or uses another model, young people and their families will most likely find that the basis of recovery involves rigorous honesty about the events in their lives, coupled with a desire to change by seeking help and building new skills to deal with the problems of life. The advantage to a program based on the twelve steps of A.A. is not only described in the process outlined by the steps, but also in providing kids and families with an automatic support group of other people with similar experiences.

A.A. steps are set on the foundation of truth, knowing what you can't change and changing what you can. The "Serenity Prayer" which is said in many treatment settings, as well as twelve-step groups, sums up this philosophy well:

God, grant me the serenity to accept the things I cannot change, the courage to change the things that I can, and the wisdom to know the difference.

The second step of A.A. talks about recognizing that our lives have not been sane and that there is someone or something out there that can help us get better. Although the steps acknowledge God, sometimes the place for kids and families to start may be with identifying other powers greater than themselves where they can receive understanding, support, and guidance. Some of these greater powers can include legal services like a probation officer, support groups, counselors familiar with addiction problems, and school and community agencies. In the first step, we recognize that there is a problem. The second step tells us that we are not alone, that there is something or someone who can help us.

In the third step of A.A., we learn that to get better, we need to surrender to the care of whatever this something or someone (Higher Power) is. The most important word in the third step is "care," because without this trust, the risks are not possible.

This philosophy suggests that chemical dependency harms us spiritually. Because of the love affair with drugs, the chemical abusers risk their relationships with other people, their Higher Power, and themselves. Although the chemical use and subsequent lifestyle meets many needs, the price is high. The unwritten rules that often accompany a chemically-oriented lifestyle include live for today; what I want comes first; authority should be defied; and if you don't get caught, it doesn't count.

Chemically-oriented lifestyles are held together with the mortar of deceit. Because of this deceit, the rules of living are very similar to the "truths" held in gangs, cults, or satanic-based groups. Kids who are in trouble with drugs are more vulnerable to some of the excitement and "living on the edge" glamour that gangs can provide. Kids who have been involved in these gang activities have more than trust or bonding issues to sort out surrounding the steps that talk about a Higher Power. If kids have only dabbled in gangs, they may be mostly concerned about whether or not God will forgive them. If they are kids who are more seriously involved with an organized gang, they may be afraid of retribution if they try to break away. They may even feel that they have gotten in too deep to turn back. These are difficult issues to work through and should be explored only with the help of professionals. Regardless of the issues that hinder an adolescent's ability to trust others and receive help, the strongest healing factor may be finding commonality with other kids. No amount of parental love can fix a chemically dependent adolescent.

The strongest recovery link seems to be in the knowledge that kids have peers who have shared some of their experiences, who like them even if they are not getting high, and who understand and relate to their confusion and pain. It is in this environment that kids find the strength to make the changes they need to get better. Recovering communities will often draw lines of similarities between themselves and the phoenix. In mythology, the phoenix rose out of its own ashes to become a thing of splendor and beauty. This is the sense that gives people in recovery hope. It is out of shared pain and despair that they find commonality, strength, and hope. It is at this point that kids may be ready to make a commitment to be chemically free.

Josh

I don't want to use anymore, but I've been getting high for so long and all of my friends get high. Sometimes I don't know if I can stop. I've started to get honest about all the things that I've done. And it hasn't been easy.

I've always felt different than other kids. I had to take special classes in school because I have a learning disability. Sometimes kids would make fun of me. I never had a lot of friends. I can remember that other kids always seemed to go to birthday parties and stuff, but I wasn't invited.

My mom and dad got divorced when I was little. My old man is a drunk. He didn't give Mom and me much money for support, so we just barely got by.

I didn't have the kind of clothes that other kids had. I didn't fit in. When I tried to talk about it to my mom once, she just said that if they didn't like me for who I was they weren't worth having as friends. She doesn't understand. So I stopped talking to her about stuff like that. I know she loves me, but she just doesn't know how I feel.

She doesn't understand why I use drugs. She thinks that I should have learned something from my dad. Well, in a way I did. I don't drink that much. I mostly smoke pot. The few times I have seen my dad, he was pretty loose. He's embarrassed me, too. One time I saw him get arrested for drunk driving. I was with my friends. It was pretty awful. But I didn't think about that stuff when I was high.

The problem is that when I was high, I did stuff that I feel bad about now. Some of the stuff is so bad I don't know if I can tell my mom and it scares me that maybe I won't be forgiven. Like once I sold this guy acid at a party. He got pretty messed up and tried to drive home on his bike and cut in front of a truck. They scraped him off the road. I went to his funeral, but I had to get stoned first.

I tried to tell myself that the reason I got high first is because Jon would have wanted it that way. You know, that the best way to honor Jon would be to go to his funeral blasted. But the real reason I got loaded was that it was the only way I could deal with it. I feel like it's my fault.

I never talked about any of this stuff before I got to treatment. I was afraid that people would hate me. I've always had a hard time making friends and I figured that if I hate myself for the things that I've done, other people would hate me, too. I remember hearing things when I was little, like "You can't expect anyone else to like you if you don't like yourself." So I figured, who could possibly like me?

Anyway, when I started to tell people about my life, I was sure that they wouldn't want anything to do with me. But I was wrong. Other kids in my group could relate to me. They couldn't relate to everything, but a lot of them felt the same way I do—lonely and scared. And some of them even had been through some of the same stuff. I thought that I was the only person who felt this way. I always thought of myself as a loser. But I don't think these other guys are losers, so maybe I'm not so bad, either.

For the first time in my life I don't feel like I'm alone. When I was with my using friends I guess I knew they didn't really care. I could never talk with them about what it was like to have a drunk for a father. None of them are writing me letters now. I think the people here really care about me. Even when they tell me something that I don't want to hear, I think it's because they care.

At first when I got here and someone would confront me, I'd get all pissed off. I'd think they were picking on me because they hated me and that they thought I was stupid. Then I'd start acting tough and try to intimidate them. But somehow things are beginning to change.

I still don't like it when people tell me I'm doing something wrong, but now I can usually stop myself and listen because I think they really do care. I know some of the kids who are here don't give a damn about getting better. Some of them are trying to con their way through. I can tell because I did that for a while, too. But some of these guys really do care. They're the ones I trust. I guess they're my friends.

For kids, much of their spirituality is expressed through their peer group. Religion may or may not be important to them. But kids come to terms with perceptions of God, forgiveness, and hope through the community of people their own age. During the teenage years, friends are more important than family members. This is the way it should be. When they were using, their values and rules were dictated by their using friends. Many attitudes were learned somewhere other than home. This is why the power of the third step comes from finding commonality with peers.

Second and Third Steps for Families

A sense of community and commonality is as important for families as it is for kids. Sometimes the best teachers are the people who have shared similar life experiences, and survived to tell about it. As the recovering addict may identify with the phoenix, the family members who share this struggle seem to identify with the metamorphosis of the butterfly. As a caterpillar, he has a life of hard work. He moves ever so slowly and is fair game for more predatory animals. He spends his time inching up never-ending trees and across fields and woods to find the right food and the right place to rest. Once he arrives, he goes about the tiresome, all-consuming job of spinning a house out of his own spit. It is only when he stops and rests that a marvelous piece of magic happens. The ugly worm turns into a graceful butterfly: a symbol of beauty and freedom.

This is the story of many families. Just being a parent can be a full-time job. Trying to control a drug-abusing teen can be thankless, tiresome, and sometimes even dangerous.

By looking at generations past, we see that parents often had the help of their extended families and community when it came to raising kids. There was almost always someone at home to deal with the matters around the house and run interference as problems arose. Before the television era, families spent their time doing something that we now need a mediator for—talking. If a crisis arose, the family (which often included aunts, uncles, and cousins) pulled together to deal with it. There was a great deal of structure provided by family, as well as community.

Not so long ago, one of the biggest problems faced by teens was cigarette smoking. Today, schools are riddled with alcohol and drugs, violence and gang activity. Teenage pregnancy is on the rise and kids worry about guns, war, and AIDS. Many young people today have experienced the loss of someone they know through violence. Many more kids have witnessed this violence first-hand. A generation ago, violent conflict mostly consisted of fist fights. Today's kids understand the terror of drive-by shootings.

From an economic standpoint, we need to acknowledge that many families need two incomes to survive. Coupled with the increasing number of single-parent households, two-income homes have created hundreds of thousands of latchkey kids. There are fewer limits for kids today, partly because there are fewer adults to hold them accountable. Families seem to suffer more from multiple crises such as divorce, adult chemical dependency, financial problems, abuse, and an unpredictable environment. And, despite all the problems that families are facing, they are getting less emotional support from extended family members and their community than at any other time in history. And even worse, it doesn't look like the situation is going to get any better in the near future.

There is no way to address all these problems with easy solutions, but something that will help more than any national drug policy is for families to pull together and unite. The isolation that families experience is, perhaps, the most difficult aspect to work with. But, like kids, families need to find common ground to heal. When we are fighting a war on drugs, doesn't it make sense to have allies with us in this fight? We wouldn't want to go into a battle by ourselves. There wouldn't be much hope of surviving, let alone winning.

I remember learning about an inner-city community that was infested with crime and poverty. The residents of that community decided they'd had enough. They banded together and started neighborhood patrols. They organized a renters' board within their housing project and laid out rules for families who wanted to live there. One of those rules was that the use of illicit drugs was prohibited. If you use, you lose! One courageous mother talked about how she was finally able to stand up to her son, who was abusing chemicals, because she didn't want to lose her home. It was clear that she had a great deal of love and support from the people close to her who were faced with the same kinds of problems.

The second and third steps show us how to begin "letting go" and offers us hope for the process of recovery. The way we receive this gift is by joining other families who share our experiences.

Bonnie

I had been to few Al-Anon meetings, but I felt really strange because it seemed like it was a place for depressed wives to go and complain about their alcoholic husbands. I had divorced my alcoholic husband years ago, so I didn't go back.

When Josh went to treatment, I didn't have much hope that he'd get any better. I was so used to disappointing reports from the school, I was afraid to get my hopes up. We started family counseling while he was in treatment and at first I would just go and listen to the lectures and try to focus on the things that didn't apply to our situation. And then I started to listen to other families as they worked with their kids in group. There were all sorts of people in those family sessions. And they were from all over, too. I didn't think I'd have much in common with any of them because they all looked so different from me. But as I listened I found that a lot of those people had similar stories and expressed feelings a lot like mine.

I remember one mother was from a very rich neighborhood. I thought we had nothing in common. She had beautiful clothes and talked about a successful husband. Then I heard her tell her son that she had planned out his death in her head. I was shocked because I had done that, too, only I thought that made me crazy. I never thought that I'd tell anyone that—not ever!

When it was my turn to work with Josh, I was terrified. I thought that the other families and counselors might tell me that I had done or not done something that caused Josh to get high. I remember telling the group that.

Josh told me things that shocked me. I was sick to hear some of what he had done while using, but at the same time I could see how much he was hurting. It had been so long since he'd talked to me about anything, let alone allowed me to look into his heart that way. I found myself filled with hope—for the first time in a long time, I felt hope.

I began to tell the others how I was feeling. I told them about how inadequate I felt as a parent. And lonely—I had been so lonely. I felt sometimes like I was the only person on the planet. And I was always terrified that other people might find out what kind of craziness I had been living with.

The other parents in the group began to talk with me about times when they felt the same way. At first I had dreaded the family counseling in treatment, but at the end I felt like it wasn't enough.

After treatment I found a Families Anonymous (F.A.) group that I was comfortable in. Then Josh came home. I thought that after Family Week everything would get better. But a week after Josh came home, he broke curfew. I had learned from the treatment counselors that I shouldn't enable him or excuse his behaviors anymore, so I grounded him for a month. After three days it felt like I was the one being punished, not Josh.

When I went to my F.A. meeting I heard a father talk about how he would get scared that his son was going to go back to using. He said, "I worried about what I would do if Nick went back to using almost every day. I would wonder what I would do until he did. Then I didn't worry anymore, I knew."

At the time I didn't know what he was talking about. But I kept going to meetings and Josh and I kept driving each other up a wall. I would make the rules and Josh would break them. I would set the consequences and then feel like I was the one doing time. But I kept at it. And the whole time Josh and I would argue. I'd tell him that things were different now, and he'd say I was being too hard and that I should just be grateful he wasn't getting high.

Then one night he came home drunk. And the funny thing is, Josh never liked to drink before that. I called the police and they took him to detox. When Josh was gone I realized that I was not only tired of fighting his battles for him, I was tired of fighting battles with him. I knew then that if he couldn't get it together, I wasn't going to go down with him. I knew I deserved some peace. And then I started to laugh because I knew what that father was talking about.

"Letting go" doesn't mean that you stop setting limits or that you "walk away" from your child. It has more to do with not holding yourself responsible for your child's behavior. It is at this point where people want advice on what kinds of limits to set. I wish I had some sure-fire plan for keeping kids chemical-free. But I don't. The second and third steps for parents aren't about what to do to get your child better. They are about what you can do to make your own life better regardless of whether or not your child recovers. Although most kids will begin to work through these steps while in treatment, families who have a child in an inpatient setting sometimes will not begin to face these issues until their child comes home. For the dependent person, "letting go" usually starts with the decision to give up the chemicals. For family members, this concept is not as easy to understand. It isn't a chemical that they have to give up, it is a behavior. Often parents will think that "letting go" means disowning their child. This option can be appealing to the parent struggling with the many issues of a chemically dependent teenager. But it is very important at this time to realize that denying the child is not the only option left to be considered. "Letting go" starts to happen for families when they begin to talk about their experiences and feelings surrounding their teen's chemical use. The process of "letting go" or "giving over" continues as they realize they are not alone, others have already experienced the same problems or similar problems, and there is hope for a brighter future.

Chapter Five

Life After Treatment

It would be nice if chemical dependency treatment were like a tonsillectomy: the patient goes in for the necessary operation, stays in the hospital for a while, then goes home "all better." Unfortunately, that's not the way it works with a chemical problem. The primary treatment is just the beginning.

"Good treatment" can only accomplish two things: it can help the young person get in touch with the seriousness of his or her chemical problem, and it can present new life options. The most challenging part of recovery happens when the young person leaves treatment. It is easier to work a first step in a controlled environment with a peer group than it is to work a first step when old using friends want the child to get high.

There are probably only two goals that any treatment experience can achieve. The first is to take apart the brick wall so that young people can honestly face what their lives have been like. In doing this, kids can realize the role that chemicals have played in their lives and get in touch with how their lives have been altered and harmed by drug use. The second goal is to then give them some new tools for dealing with life without using chemicals. This is to give them hope, because when you take away something as powerful as drugs and a drug-oriented lifestyle, something needs to be put in its place. With the accomplishment of these goals, the young person is ready for aftercare. Aftercare can be either in an outpatient setting or a residential setting (halfway house, extended care, or group home). The kids learn to apply the skills that they learned in treatment in the aftercare center.

Prior to discharge, the complete aftercare plan should be discussed with both the parents and child. Alcoholics Anonymous or Narcotics Anonymous will most likely be recommended for the child. A twelve-step family support group will probably be recommended for parents. These support groups are a vital part of the recovery process. Follow-up studies show that the quality of recovery is directly proportional to a solid aftercare plan. Many times, family involvement is required. If there are other issues that need attention (abuse, depression, unresolved grief), a secondary referral for private counseling or a specialized support group may be made. Aftercare plans differ and are sometimes limited by available community resources. Regardless of what was recommended, it is important to follow through. The time following treatment is likely to be unstable.

More than once I have seen kids sabotage their recoveries because success was too scary. This is another reason that following through with aftercare plans are so critical. The objective support of an experienced professional can help kids and families through these troubling times. This may sound like more hard work—it is. Recovery for kids and families isn't easy, but then, neither was living with them when they were using drugs. The support from your twelve-step group and sponsor, aftercare agency, and the child's sponsor may be all that gets you through the first few months.

Six to ten weeks following treatment, kids go through a grieving process. The same kinds of emotions that you might feel when someone you love has died are experienced when kids reenter the community. This is because they are grieving their old friends, their way to socialize, and their chemicals. Most importantly, kids grieve the identity that they used to have while they were drinking and getting high. Many times, immediately after their treatment, kids experience a "treatment high." They feel a sense of euphoria as a result of the hard work they have done and the progress they have made. Many kids report that their treatment experience was the first thing they were able to feel good about in a long time. When they complete treatment, they often think that everything else in their life will be new and different. They may want to share their experience with everyone and anyone who will listen. They are somewhat like converts to a religion.

A few hours to a few weeks later, the "high" starts to wear off. Kids start to get in touch with the fact that even if they are clean and sober, many things in their world are the same. They start to realize that school is still a drag, that their families still have conflict, and that some of the painful issues in their lives still hurt.

One young man struggling through this very stressful time told me, "I thought that being straight was lousy. I guess it's life that's lousy." In one sense he was right. Sometimes life is lousy. Sometimes life is hard, and sometimes life is just unfair. Part of living is knowing how to handle pain and that "this too shall pass."

This is a hard realization for kids because they are focused on living in the present. It is especially hard for kids with chemical abuse problems because they not only live in the present, they are used to dealing with problems by getting a "quick fix." When reality sets in, the grieving process begins.

During this time it is typical for kids to go backward. They often recycle old defenses in an attempt to rebuild the brick wall because these patterns are more familiar than the new behaviors they learned in treatment. Many times kids will try to find a way out by saying, "I really don't think that I have a problem with my drugs because I exaggerated my use in treatment just to fit in." Don't be alarmed if your child says this. Arguing with the child or trying to prove that he or she does have a problem will be futile. But stand firm on your expectations about chemicals.

Often when kids start to flirt with denial, they are truly missing what the using life-style offered them. Just because they have gone through treatment does not mean that the world has changed. It is hard for kids to see their old friends party and use and have a good time. Adolescents who are new in recovery often have little else with which to compare life. They know that they cannot go backward and be where they were before they began using. It is important for parents to realize this, too. If the child was really complete before he or she started to use, the child would not have gotten into trouble with chemicals in the first place. The early phases of recovery can be lonely, scary times.

Another common sign of this grief is bargaining. Many times kids will say something like, "My problem was acid and hash. I never had any problems with alcohol. I think I can drink now." This kind of thinking is very dangerous for kids because it sounds almost logical. But kids need to be reminded that they weren't addicted to the chemical, but to the high. Very few kids are physically addicted to substances. For those who are, once they have completed treatment, any remnants of the physical cravings are long gone. They miss the good feeling and the high, their friends and the "fun times." They miss who they thought they were.

When they were getting high, kids knew where they fit in; they knew how they could make friends. When the drugs and the drug-oriented lifestyle are gone, kids find themselves feeling empty and lost. While they were in treatment, they were surrounded by other kids who were going through those same kinds of issues. When they return to the community, they find there are people in the world who don't care and don't want to care. Because adolescents are so dependent on the approval of their peers, they will sometimes scramble to find a way to regain this approval.

Following the denial and bargaining, many kids will show anger. They are angry at their parents and whoever else got in the way of their use. They are angry at themselves for not feeling any better, and they are angry at the world because it didn't change when they did. Feelings of "why me?" can prevail.

Beyond the anger is sadness. Some kids will even have symptoms of depression, which include lethargy, fatigue, and disturbances in patterns of sleeping or eating. (If your child demonstrates any of these symptoms, have him or her assessed by a qualified professional.)

The grief process varies from one individual to another. Some kids will exhibit these symptoms several times during this phase of recovery.

During this period of time their ability to abstain may be fragile, and relapses can occur. There is nothing that you can do to stop these feelings. In fact, to move on, kids need to go through this grieving process. However, realize that when a child is going through this trying time, he or she needs consistent, predictable rules. Being sensitive to your child's pain is quite different than enabling behaviors. These kids cannot go back to who they were before they began to use. Too much has happened.

Many times kids will express frustration because they feel misunderstood by their families, who are also grieving. They sense that their families want the "little kid back." In many cases this is true. As much as kids grieve, so do families. Parents may want to forget about what happened and start all over. This is not practical or fair. One of the promises of recovery is "We will not forget the past, nor wish to shut the door on it."

One way young people in recovery can begin to feel pride is by staying in touch with some of the things that caused shame. Old unhealthy behaviors act as a yardstick with which to measure their progress. When kids realize they have changed some of these behaviors and patterns, they can begin to let go of their "using" identity.

Some people believe that kids stop growing emotionally when they begin to abuse drugs. If this is true, kids are not only grieving their old way of life, they are also playing "catch up" with their emotional development. Once the grief begins to subside (sometime around the third month of recovery), kids can begin building a different identity for themselves. This is hard work, but it is also a time of exploration and renewal.

Being free from drugs does not mean kids are free from being adolescents. Even without the drugs, kids are apt to be self-centered, concrete in their thinking, and rebellious. This is the nature of adolescence. Chemically dependent kids are going to spend a little extra time in that developmental phase. As they become reacquainted with themselves, family members can take the opportunity to get to know them as well.

Linda

When Jenny came home from treatment we were all pretty nervous. At first it seemed like it was too good to be true—and it was. Jenny's first few days were pretty much spent at home with Joe and me. We went shopping and to a movie her first weekend out and had some great talks. It felt like my little girl was back and everything in the past three years was only a bad dream.

Jenny was terrified to go back to school, but we didn't want to prolong the inevitable. She'd missed so much school already. At first she was just nervous. But after being back a few weeks, she seemed to get downright withdrawn. I wanted to enroll her in another school, but Joe said that we should let her decide if that was what she wanted. When we asked her about it, she just snapped.

"Why do you always have to mess with my life?" she yelled.

"We're just trying to talk about this, baby," I said. "We want to make it easier for you."

"I'm not a baby!" she screamed at me. "Nothing is going to make it easier for me. My life is ruined. Nobody likes me anymore. They all think I'm a narc. I hate my life and I hate you for messing with it in the first place!" Then she ran to her room.

I felt trapped and alone.

We made sure that she continued to go to her aftercare groups, and we went, too. Her sponsor got her to and from A.A., but I was terrified that we were going to lose her again. Then one day she came home and announced that she could socially use again.

"How could you possibly believe that?" Joe said to her. "You've only been straight for twelve weeks— and five of those weeks you were in treatment."

"I think my problems were more related to emotions," she said, "and now that I've learned how to express my feelings, I think I'll be able to drink without any consequences."

"Not in my house," I said. "If you decide that's what you want to do, you're going to have to wait

until you've moved out. There's no way we're going through that craziness again."

That was the beginning of Round Two. That lasted for an eternity. She began to call her old friends. We found out that she'd begun to cut some classes, too. Joe and I were terrified that she'd started to use again. The counselor suggested house arrest and more limits with closer supervision. Then he told her that if she could not live by our rules, he'd help us find a residential aftercare for her, like a group home or a halfway house. Jenny just about took his head off. But I think she was really scared. She could see that her father and I were together on this—and that was something she wasn't used to.

The next few weeks weren't easy on any of us. Joe and I didn't give Jenny much leeway, and I know her aftercare group was on her pretty hard, too. But, we got through it. When she got her six-month pin she seemed to be a little better. She wasn't testing rules so much at home, but she seemed to be withdrawn again. When I finally asked her about it, she began to cry.

"Mom," she said, "I don't know where I fit in at school. I really want to be straight, really! But it's just so hard. I keep hearing all my old friends talk about the great parties they are going to. Some of them ignore me and some of them try to get me to go with them. They say things like, 'You could just come and drink Pepsi or something.' And, Mom, I really want to—except that I know it wouldn't be any fun if I couldn't get high with them. I just don't know who I am anymore. I'm so lonely and *bored." And then she just sobbed.*

I held her so long I thought she might never move. I didn't know what to say. I asked her what we could do. She said, "Nothing."

Later, she called her sponsor and they went out. I don't know what happened at the meeting, but it sure helped. Things got better slowly. We still have our ups and downs. Jenny has a mind of her own and she still likes to test Joe and I. I guess she does that just to make sure we aren't sleeping on the job.

Jenny's been clean for eight months now. She still wears tattered jeans, and you wouldn't believe what she did to her hair last week! We still argue, and every once in a while she storms off to her room. But we talk, too. It's not all very easy to listen to, but she seems to know how much I can handle. We're beginning to have fun together, too! She sure isn't the same little girl who used to be in Girl Scouts. But she isn't the same unpredictable, scary stranger who lived here nine months ago, either.

Are We Getting Better Yet?

Families in recovery go through a process. Getting healthy doesn't happen all at once. Here are some signs that you are on your way.

Recognizing the Truth

Often, parents of a chemically abusive child are unable to distinguish truth from lies. They have been living with a drug abuser who has become adept at manipulating the truth to suit his or her purposes. Because parents want to believe their child, they become more and more distrustful of their own instincts and intuition. When parents regain the ability to see untruths and can once more trust their intuition, they regain some lost power.

Goodbye to the Guilts

Guilt seems to come with the job of being the parent of a chemically dependent child. Parents feel guilty for the things they have done and for the things they haven't done. Kids seem to be experts at knowing just when and how to set a torch to the guilt that smolders within their parents. When parents start to set consistent limits and take back their parenting power, they quickly learn that they are not going to win any popularity contest with their kids—especially when these kids are used to running their own lives and having their way. The goal for parents is to set limits without feeling guilty. A more realistic expectation might be to stick to the limits, with or without guilt.

Forgiveness

When we talk about forgiveness, we must look at letting go of the pain and anger we feel toward our children, and of the disappointment we have in ourselves. To do this, we must have permission to grieve. Part of healing is saying goodbye to what was.

Forgiveness comes in pieces—it doesn't happen all at once. It goes hand in hand with trust. And trust must be rebuilt. It will take parents a while to trust their child again—that is all right. Remember, the child hasn't demonstrated good decision-making skills. "Proving" themselves is part of their healing process. It may also take some time for parents to trust themselves again. Be patient. As long as there are signs of forgiveness happening, things are headed in the right direction.

Making Mistakes

Chemical abuse is a serious problem. The pain and destruction it causes can leave a family feeling torn and shattered. Recovery is often painful, too. By looking at old hurts, we relive the pain. But part of getting better is being able to laugh at ourselves. There is an incredible amount of healing that happens when we stop taking everything so seriously. Now, there are some things that need direct, no-nonsense attention, and you will make mistakes along the way. That's good. It means you're trying new things (let's face it, the old approaches didn't work). Mistakes breed creativity. And if you have a kid who has been in trouble with drugs, you are going to need creativity in your parenting style. Learn to laugh at your mistakes.

Ed

When Jan was getting high, I was going crazy. I used to spy on her and set all sorts of limits and expectations even a saint couldn't follow. Then when she'd have a crisis, she'd always bring up how I was never really there for her. So I'd try to pay restitution by buying her nice things.

When Jan went to treatment, I was sure that her counselor was going to tell me, "Ed, if you were a better father, Jan wouldn't get high," but that didn't happen. Instead of learning what made Jan use drugs, I learned how my own behaviors made me sick. I began to realize that my need to control Jan is probably one reason I have an ulcer.

I was terrified of having her come home. At first, I found myself listening to her phone conversations and interrogating any new, straight friends she brought home. Jan hated me for this, but I needed to feel like I had some control.

About a month after she was home, she gave me some story about staying overnight with her sponsor. Until that point, even though I watched her like a hawk, I also believed what she was telling me. But this time it didn't feel right. When I called her sponsor, I found out she had no clue about Jan's plan. I confronted Jan and she came back at me with all the same things that I felt guilty about. "You're never there for me," she said. "You didn't trust me. You just want to catch me screwing up so you can feel good." I almost backed down because for the hundredth time I felt like a lousy father.

But I didn't back down. Instead, I grounded her for a year. Later, at the Tough Love meeting, I told the group about my actions. "Gee, Ed," said another member, "don't you think you're being a little permissive? Jan's fourteen years old. Why don't you ground her until she's an adult?" Everyone laughed—and I had to laugh, too. Later, I adjusted her consequence and told her I was scared to lose her again.

Over the past six months, my intuitions have gotten better. I don't feel a need to be her watchdog so much. She's changed, and so have I. I think we both trust each other a little more. When I go back to being obsessive, there is always someone in my group to point that out. They've lovingly dubbed me "The Count of Control."

Limits vs. Control

When you are getting reacquainted with your child, you may find times when you'll wish you didn't know him or her. If you find yourself feeling this way, you're not alone. We are taught to look for "progress, not perfection." Looking for progress in someone with whom you set limits can be quite a challenge. Progress does not always mean that you are on an uphill climb with your child. Sometimes it means that there will be setbacks and that progress will need to be measured in how you get back on track.

Your kids aren't the only ones going through changes, either. You may find yourself slipping into old patterns of thinking and behaving. Serenity can be evasive. By having consistent limits, expectations, and consequences, you may have an edge. If you and your child know ahead of time what the rules are, you will not find yourself overreacting during an emotional crisis.

Consequences for unacceptable behavior should be unpleasant. If your kid doesn't mind the punishment, then it isn't a consequence. Different things are important to different kids. Find out what is important to your child. As parents, we make sure our children are fed, clothed, and have a safe place to live. These human rights should never be compromised when devising an appropriate measure for unacceptable behavior. Twelve-step meetings and phone calls to the sponsor should not be considered privileges. These are some examples of privileges that can be pulled for breaking rules:

- Television, music/stereo
- Phone privileges (with the exception of calling the sponsor)
- Outside privileges (with the exception of school, A.A./N.A., or an outing with the family)
- Transportation (car/bike)
- Video games
- Having friends over
- Special planned events (parties/group activities)

- Reverse room restriction (the child cannot hang out alone or be isolated in his or her room)

If you give your child permission to go to a twelve-step meeting while he or she is on house restrictions, tell your child to be home directly after the meeting.

Other parents who have similar experiences can offer you ideas and support. You don't have to take this task on alone. When enforcing a consequence, it may be a good idea to establish a time limit. Anything beyond one week winds up punishing the rest of the family more than the offending adolescent. Discuss time limits before the rule is broken. If a major rule is broken or the offense is repeated, give more than one consequence.

Many kids demonstrate their progress by taking two steps forward and one step backward. This is especially true of kids who have a well-established cycle of self-defeating behaviors. Once these kids come down from their treatment high, they tend to feel overwhelmed and fearful.

Sometimes more insightful adolescents will report a sense of impending doom. Often they are not finished working through the pain of their own poor self-concept. Success still feels foreign to these kids. Recognizing their worth may not be enough.

Stop the Ride! I Want to Get Off!

Living with a child who has a drug problem is scary for everyone in the family. Recovery, especially the early months, is most often filled with turmoil as well. The emotional highs and lows experienced by each person puts the family on a runaway roller coaster. Kids who have grown up around chaos become used to a certain level of "craziness" in their homes. It may sound strange, but these kids often feel that the unpredictable conflict they have experienced is a normal thing. As soon as one child starts making progress, it is not unusual for another child to begin having problems. Sometimes kids do this because discord feels normal to them, others are just demonstrating behaviors they know will get them attention because they are feeling left out.

Rick

Since Jamie came home from treatment, I feel like I have a new career as a plate spinner. I can't give all my attention to Jamie, even though that's what I seem to want to do. I am so afraid that she will start using again, that I spend a lot of time focusing on her. I did this when she was getting high, too. The difference is that now, I want to concentrate on how she is changing, you know—doing better. Her brother and two sisters were used to Jamie being the "problem child." One time her older sister, Amber, pointed this out to me. I can remember her saying, "What do I have to do to get you to spend time with me? Maybe I should smoke some crack, crash a car, and rob you blind. Then when I stopped being a jerk, you'd see that I live here, too."

What an eye-opener that was. It was like I was so proud of Jamie, I had forgotten that I have three other kids who don't have a drug problem. So now I'm the plate-spinning dad. I give Jamie a spin, then I look to see who needs me next and I give that one a spin. With four kids, it's a lot of time. But I guess that's what being a parent is about—spending time with your kids.

Chapter Six

The Need for Highs: Relapses and Cross-Addictions

Even with a strong effort toward recovery, some families and kids return to unhealthy and self-destructive behaviors. Sometimes this culminates in a relapse or a cross-addiction.

Some literature suggests that all these problems are rooted in different issues. I disagree. People with addictions suffer from the basic problem of a poor self-concept that borders on self-hate. Because they do not feel good about who they are, they find something that can make them feel better about themselves. This something can be chemicals, sex, gambling, eating (or not eating), or other people.

Nobody likes pain, but dependent individuals seem to have a very low threshold for pain—perhaps because they have found ways to get a "quick fix." The drug dependence produces a state of euphoria in which problems are diminished or completely disappear. For kids who have experienced painful events, this can be manna from heaven.

When the drugs are taken away, these kids can feel stripped and vulnerable. Sometimes their new skills aren't enough to combat the hurts that pursue them. It is then that these kids run the risk of relapse, or developing another set of unhealthy addictive behaviors.

This does not mean that all of the work in treatment has been wasted. Nor does it mean that you have to start all over in another kind of treatment experience. Relapses and cross-addictions do not happen overnight. Here are some predictable signs:

- isolation (withdrawing from family and support networks)
- arrogance/denial (believing they no longer need help—that they are "cured")

The behaviors that go along with these warning signs include:

- getting in touch with old using friends
- violating set rules with little or no regard for the consequences of their actions
- dishonesty

Dishonesty is the strongest sign of impending or certain relapse. These symptoms are visible during the grief period of early recovery. During these times they are at high risk for relapse.

Later in the grieving process (after three to nine months of sobriety), the reccurrence of these signals should be cause for concern. When kids become comfortable with chemical-free lifestyles, they can address underlying life traumas. We "fall apart" when we are safe enough and healthy enough to do so. In other words, we get well at our own rates, and getting well means that we may get in touch with old pains. Some of these old pains may have been buried or forgotten.

While in treatment and early recovery, kids can only do so much. Underlying issues may have been identified but not resolved. Later in recovery, it is crucial for them to go back and pay closer attention to these unresolved issues. It is not uncommon for kids to block painful memories until they can deal with them. Some defenses are healthy. Kids who are more prone to relapses and cross-addictions are the kids who have work to do to address these underlying problems.

Some relapse literature written for kids is based on an adult model. This is not very useful. It presumes that adolescent drug abuse is the same as adult drug abuse. I do not believe that is true. Teenage substance abuse is more about the development of unhealthy survival skills. Trying to adapt an adult treatment model for kids does not suit their needs. Focusing on relapse warning signs only moves many kids further away from the issues that underlay their chemical abuse. When kids resume their using lifestyle, it is because chemicals are meeting a need for them that wasn't met in another manner. We must intervene and identify the issues that the adolescent has been struggling with. When kids use chemicals to medicate painful life events, they have a difficult time sorting through the painful feelings that arise. Some traumatic life events take a long time to heal. Although traditional aftercare and twelve-step groups can address some of these issues, additional support from a clinician may be necessary (such as rape counseling or grief support). If specialized counseling is needed, find a clinician who is familiar with chemical dependency and who can work with the support network already in place. Be aware that some clinicians will not see someone who is new in recovery. This is because many counselors believe that gaining a strong foothold on being sober is crucial before delving into other problems. Cross-addictions are nothing more than another form of relapse. The young person still does not have the stability to progress beyond a certain point in recovery, even though he or she may have made a very strong commitment to avoid chemicals.

We all need avenues through which we can feel good about ourselves or "in control." In the best situations, these good feelings are a result of close, interpersonal relationships and our personal and collective accomplishments. For kids who are in trouble with drugs, this isn't the case. Kids either don't have the skills necessary to form close, interpersonal relationships, or they have such a negative self-view, that they cannot take ownership of their accomplishments. The crises they create are attempts at survival. It is out of these crises that cross-addictions occur.

Suzanne

After treatment, I really wanted to do well. My mom is recovering, too, so I thought that we would really be good for each other—like best friends or something. I remember her telling me how hard it would be sometimes, but I had no idea that it would be this hard.

After I was home about a month, things seemed to get worse and worse. I hated school and I missed getting high. My little brother and sister started to get on my nerves. I didn't feel like I had any kind of life and my mom had turned into Miss A.A. of America. She seemed like she was really getting into it, and I felt lonely and miserable. To be honest, I was jealous, too. I didn't feel like I was good at anything. I went into this really big pity trip and quit going to A.A. It wasn't long after that that I got stinking, falling down, throwing up, sloppy drunk. My mom handled it pretty well, but I felt lousy.

I tried to get more serious about aftercare and A.A. because I knew that I didn't ever want to go back to using again. But nothing seemed to help. I kept getting more and more unhappy. And I wound up gaining fifteen pounds. That made things even worse. I felt ugly and gross.

Then I met this guy at A.A. He started to pay attention to me and that felt good. I didn't feel good about my body, so I started to go on this crash diet and even started to make myself throw up. The attention from Jay and losing the weight made me feel like I was in control.

It wasn't long before Jay and I were having sex, and that was really pretty hard for me. I didn't feel like I was ready for that, but I was afraid to lose him. So I did it. It wasn't like I was a virgin or anything. I'd had boyfriends when I was using. But I'd never been in a relationship that didn't involve using, too.

After a few weeks, we started having arguments and that really made me scared. I wanted Jay to spend more time with me and I was jealous of his other friends. He said I was suffocating him. We started to fight more and more. I was terrified of losing him. We had sex more often. I thought that would keep me from losing him. I started to eat more, too, but I was scared of getting fat so I threw up more. I was miserable.

Then one day my sponsor sat me down and told me that she was worried about me. She said I looked terrible and that she thought Jay was using me. I cried and cried. She asked me what was wrong and I told her that I hated myself, that I didn't like having sex, but I was afraid to lose Jay. I told her what I'd been doing with my eating. She held me for a long time and then she said that I'd need to tell my mom and get some help or she would tell her for me. I was so scared. But then I decided to tell my mom because nothing seemed like it was working for me.

My sponsor was with me when I talked to my mom and that really helped. My mom was calmer than I thought she'd be. She called my aftercare counselor to make an appointment to bring me in the next day for a private session. When I was talking to my counselor she said that she had reviewed my chart from treatment. She asked me if I thought there might be some things that I needed more help with—things that were making me feel bad about myself. I told her I didn't think so. Then she said that she knew I had been abused by one of my mother's boyfriends when I was little. At first I was pissed, and I said, "I've already talked about that. It doesn't bother me anymore."

"How do you feel about your body?" she asked. "About sex?"

I felt like my stomach was up in my throat. Everything around me was all cloudy and gray. We talked a little longer and then she said that she thought I should see someone who knew a lot about abuse. I was both mad and scared because I felt like I was broken and that I'd never get any better. That was two months ago.

Things still aren't great, but I don't feel like everything is falling in on me anymore. Jay and I broke up and I feel kind of insecure and lonely. But I'm not doing things that make me feel worse about who I am.

◆◆◆

In Suzanne's case, underlying abuse issues seemed to contribute to her self-destructive behaviors on several levels. Her counselor was able to help her make the connection between her abuse, her feelings about her body, and her sexuality. Whether she was medicating feelings with alcohol, food, or sex, the end result was the same—Suzanne was looking for a way to regain a sense of control when she was feeling particularly vulnerable.

Not all kids are able to identify their problems as easily as she did. Some kids have more difficulty bonding and may also be less insightful. Regardless of their issues, how kids feel about themselves is reflected in their behaviors. How kids act will tell us more than what they say. Most often, young people will not ask directly for help. But if they don't have a strong support network, their actions will let us know. Many kids who are in trouble with drugs have limited emotional and cognitive development. When a young person's behaviors indicate that he or she is not doing well, parents and interested adults must share their concerns with the young person.

Early in recovery and at crisis times (painful life events or life changes), young people are at risk of resuming old or unhealthy addictive behaviors. These behaviors are an attempt to survive or get through the crisis. It is important for us not to get bogged down in the addictive behavior itself, but recognize that the behavior is meeting an emotional need for the child.

Early intervention following treatment is crucial. Letting things slide will almost certainly make them worse. For families, it is difficult to know when to "let go." It is even difficult to give a solid definition of what "letting go" means. Because the parent-child relationship is different than the adult-adult relationship, it is more difficult to determine when, or if, there is a time to sever the bond. There are no correct solutions to this very difficult problem. Whether or not the child gets any better is more up to the child than it is to the parent.

Chapter Seven

Prevention: Myth vs. Fact

Although this book is primarily about kids in trouble with drugs, a question I've often heard from families is "What can we do about the younger siblings?" What I have discussed up until now presumes an already established problem with chemicals. Although adolescent drug abuse seems to be on the rise, it is not realistic to assume that all kids using chemicals wind up abusing them or become addicted. Therefore, understanding prevention techniques can be a useful parenting tool. Experimenting with alcohol and other drugs is often a rite of passage for young people today. Some kids can experiment with chemical use and are able to draw the line where "enough is enough." Some kids will even start to develop an unhealthy pattern of use and be able to pull away from this lifestyle before it gets out of control.

Much of what is labeled as prevention in our society today is not much more than a slick, ineffective ad campaign. Slogans like "Just Say No" seem to avoid what the real prevention issues are. However, it is ludicrous to believe that just saying no is prevention. It is difficult, if not impossible, for many kids to say no to drugs. If we review what chemicals do for kids, such as providing a social outlet, offering a means to cope with painful feelings and problems, creating a sense of courage and confidence, and offering an instant sense of identity, then it's easy to see why just saying no is so hard for many young people today.

If we examine chemical use as a rite of passage in our culture, we can understand the power of a well-produced advertisement for alcohol. The producer is giving the message that drinking their particular brew will make us happier, sexier, and more popular. Many ads on television today look a lot like music videos. They appeal to kids on a fantasy level. One commercial shows a young man creating snow from a beer billboard on a sweltering day, bringing the gratitude of several beautiful young women. Another ad features a red dog talking (with the voice of a celebrity) about what is cool. Daily, we see alcohol ads clearly aimed toward the young. The ad executives know exactly what they are doing. They know their market of the future lies in our children. Does a red bulldog really have a strong appeal for the "over thirty" crowd? Our young people are conditioned from a very early age to view alcohol and drug use as a significant part of "growing up." When our young people are saturated with these ads on television, I sometimes think that they must find adults who preach "Just Say No" to be somewhat ridiculous. Everything else they have learned has taught them to "Just Say Yes."

Scared Straight

Another tactic that I believe is relatively useless in prevention is the "scare tactic." One public service commercial says, "One way to get you message across is to use famous people in your ad." The commercial then shows stills of celebrities who died of drug overdoses. As an adult and a parent I find this message chilling. But we must remember that adolescents do not believe in their own mortality. They live in the present and see themselves as invincible. Seeing dead celebrities on the television is not as powerful as seeing the friends they grew up with get high and have a good time.

This kind of prevention is nothing new. It is supposed to scare kids so they will not want to use drugs. In the early 1970s, a police officer came to my school to employ the same sort of tactics when I was in eleventh grade. He told us some horrible stories about kids who got high and wound up in accidents with their "brains splattered everywhere." Next he showed us a movie in which a young man got high before he went to his job as a mechanic. The young man was supposed to fix the brakes on a woman's car, but was too stoned to do it right. When the woman was driving on a treacherous stretch of road and tried to slow down, she realized she had no brakes. She lost control of the car and went shooting off the side of the cliff, plummeting to her death. When the movie was over, the police officer addressed us again. He recapped the movie in his most hair raising, awe-inspiring voice, and asked "Did you learn anything?" My friend Jack (who had gotten high with me before the drug presentation) leaned over to me and said, "Yeah, I learned that if you're going to get high, you shouldn't be a mechanic. You should do something more natural, like raising dope."

The moral of the story is that scare tactics only work in the kids who are already scared. Since teens don't generally sense their own mortality, trying to scare them with something that might (or might not) happen to them is not an effective form of prevention. Scare tactics don't seem to have a lasting impression on younger kids, either. Follow up studies have shown that the D.A.R.E. program in elementary schools (sponsored by police to keep kids off drugs) has no effect on preventing drug abuse with these same children once they are in junior high or high school. Although young children may be impressed, they may change their minds when they see friends and acquaintances experiment with alcohol and drugs.

Geoff

I saw a commercial on television that said drugs are bad. It said things like, "Why do you think they call it dope," and stuff like that. We had some drug education in school, too. They told us all about the bad stuff that can happen to you if you get high. Well, the problem with that was, I already knew more about getting high than they talked about. My older brother got high all the time. Sometimes I hated him because he would be such a jerk to my mom, but I liked him a lot, too. Sometimes he would let me hang around him and his friends—a lot of the time, they even acted like I was one of them. I thought that was pretty cool. And besides, other than how my brother treated my mom, I didn't see anything terrible happening to him like the stuff they show on T.V. or talk about in school. I guess I decided early on that some of that stuff was just trash. When I was ten, my brother and his friends got me high for the first time. It was great. I felt so good and nothing bad happened.

◆◆◆

The best prevention ad I've seen on television is the one where the father confronts his son with drugs that he has found. He screams at his son, "Who taught you about this?"

The son is resistant to answer at first, but finally replies, "You—I learned it by watching you." This commercial has a powerful statement for us. Our society is full of double messages about drug and alcohol use. After thirty seconds of a beer ad filled with young and beautiful people having an outrageously good time, laughing and partying and drinking and flirting, we hear a three second disclaimer that says, "Know when to say when." Which message do you think has the strongest impact on impressionable young minds?

Looking at Ourselves

We are a society that claims to be concerned about the drug problem in our nation, especially among young people, and yet we are a society that is obsessed with drugs. Recently, I watched a documentary on television about the drug problem in America. The documentary bothered me for several reasons. First of all, the majority of people interviewed and depicted were people of color. If I were to believe the documentary, I would believe that the drug problem in our country was with crack cocaine and that the problem centered in the Hispanic and African-American communities of the inner cities. Although this is a real part of the drug problem, it is an unfair and biased view that perpetuates the myth that drugs are only a problem with minorities, the poor, or the underprivileged. This kind of mentality seems to feed the denial that our nation has been feasting on for the past decade. We must all recognize that chemical abuse crosses socio-economic and racial barriers.

Another disturbing thing about this documentary was the list of sponsors. Included were an analgesic company, a brewery, and a major producer of coffee. Now you may say that these chemicals seem relatively harmless. But I believe the larger message is that we are a country that is obsessed with feeling good. If your back hurts, take a pill. Tired? Wake up to some good coffee. Do you want to lose weight? There's something for that, too. We seem to be in endless pursuit of the perfect life—free of pain, problems, and unsightly cellulite. We are encouraged to take something for headaches, something else for PMS, something else for tooth pain, another something else for backaches, hemorrhoids, sleeplessness, fatigue, weight loss, and on and on. I think again of the ad where the young man tells his father that he learned to use drugs "by watching you," and I feel a little guilty. Young America has learned about taking drugs from us in more ways than one. Perhaps the message from this ad needs to be understood on two levels. The most obvious level is that parents certainly do model behaviors about acceptable drug use to children through their relationship with drugs. But perhaps the bigger message is to us as a nation. We are a people who intensely dislike any form of discomfort and we are in an endless pursuit of something that will make us feel better.

It is not my intention to blame anyone for our young people's drug problems, but I think it is necessary to be objective about the world we live in if we are going to be able to make any changes.

Believing the stereotypes and myths perpetuated by the media about chemical abuse seems to be half the problem. I remember a young woman who I worked with several years ago who was having a hard time coming to terms with the fact that she had wound up in a chemical dependency treatment program. Although she acknowledged that she had been using drugs daily, had suffered numerous blackouts and had been hospitalized for an accidental overdose, she still couldn't believe that she "was the kind of person who could have a problem with drugs." Frustrated, she told her group, "You guys just don't understand! I don't have problems in my life like you do! I listen to other people in here and I feel sort of guilty, because my life isn't so bad. I know that I fight with my parents, but I also know that they both love me. I have almost everything I've ever wanted, I go to a private school and my grades aren't even that bad. People like me just don't wind up having a problem with drugs. It's only people who live in the ghetto who have drug problems."

Prevention with an Impact

One of the basic problems that exists with "Just Say No" is that it assumes that the problem we need to begin with is the chemicals themselves. This is not true, because that is where the problem ends, not where it begins. We need to talk about what is behind the chemical abuse problem. And that means looking at some pretty scary issues and being ready to talk about some pretty hard topics with our kids.

Earlier in this book, we examined some traumatic life events that are commonly linked to adolescent chemical abuse. I know it's impossible to wrap our kids in a cocoon and shelter them from harm. Sometimes even the best parent can say or do hurtful things. And sometimes unfair and traumatic things happen to people when they are too young to know how to handle them. As parents, we cannot stop these things from happening, but we can create a safe environment in which our children can express who they are and what they need. If you think your child may be at risk for chemical abuse because of unresolved trauma, the best advice I can give you is to start talking about it.

Parents as Role Models

An unfair assumption in our culture is that parents are supposed to have all the answers. T.V. role model families (the Cleavers, Bradys,

Huxtables, Taylors from *Home Improvement,* and so on) don't seem to make bad parenting decisions that have a negative affect on their kids. If they do make mistakes, they do not seem to compare to some of the blunders I have pulled. I think some of my best parenting has come when I have apologized to my son when I have been wrong. I think it helps him to see that Mom is human and that she screws up, and that it's okay to screw up sometimes. Building self-esteem in our children is an important job that we have to take seriously. The most important thing we can do for our kids is to pay attention to how we treat ourselves. The best prevention is going to come from families pulling together and being families. After all, we are our kid's first and most important role models. Being a role model is an important job. It means that we have to examine our own behaviors and our own values, both the spoken and unspoken. What is the message that we are giving our kids if they see us drinking? I am not suggesting that everybody has to be abstinent all the time, but I think we have to look carefully at the examples we set. Do our kids see us taking pills? What are the messages we give them about how to handle problems or conflict? Are there unspoken rules in the house about what is okay to talk about and what we leave unsaid? We need to pay attention to how we treat each other. Are we respectful? Do all family members have a right to their feelings? What happens if someone makes a mistake? Is there forgiveness? I'm not sure there are any set of correct answers to these questions, but perhaps what is most important is asking the questions in the first place.

After we acknowledge that our behavior influences our children's view of us, as well as themselves, we need to address the never-ending job of helping our kids to build a positive sense of self. This can be difficult because we are not the only ones to affect our children. We must spend time with our kids, doing things with them that are important to them, and talking with them about the things that they are interested in. Get to know them by recognizing what they think makes them important or unique. Listen to their problems. But be careful not to try to solve their problems for them. Kids need to learn that sometimes life hurts, that there are no quick fixes. Help them find things they do well and feel good about, and support the pursuit of these activities. This takes commitment.

And last, but not least, set limits. Kids need to know that there are rules and they need to know exactly what the rules are. When behaviors are unacceptable, they need to know exactly what will happen to them. Be prepared, kids will break rules—that's their job.

If rules and expectations are inconsistent, you can bet that your kids will be confused, and confused kids tend to test limits more often and with amazing zeal because they aren't convinced that the rules make sense. Kids learn this at a very early age.

When my son Preston was four years old, he taught me a lot about how persistent a child can be. My son was probably no different than 99 percent of all of our children. He, like his peers, hated to go to bed. He was always this way. He seemed to be afraid that he'd miss something. Because he had to be up at 6:00 A.M. on weekdays, his bedtime had to be no later than 8:00 P.M. so that he would be human while at day care the next day. But while my husband Charles was on a week-long hunting trip, Preston decided to see just how set his bedtime was.

It was Sunday night and Preston was bathed and tucked into bed. At 8:05, I heard his wailing cries. Alarmed, I rushed to his room to see what was troubling him.

"I miss Daddy!" he cried.

Feeling angry at my husband for taking a week's vacation from parenting and guilty because somehow I was "not enough," I allowed Preston to get up and watch "a little T.V." It was 9:00 before he fell asleep on the couch. The next day he behaved like a small toad at day care.

That night I had Preston bathed and tucked in at 8:00, feeling certain he would be tired enough to fall sleep. (Sometimes I think that the real reason we have children is so we can get in touch with just how little we actually know.) At 8:03, he was whooping and wailing again. I could hear his pathetic cries of "I miss Daddy! I miss Daddy!" before I even got to his room. This time I was determined to be the firm parent.

"Go to sleep, Preston," I said in my best grown-up mother's voice. "You can't get back up. You have school tomorrow and you need to sleep."

Preston didn't miss a beat. He sucked in one of those choking sobs and cried, "But I miss Daddy . . . (sob) . . . I'm afraid he'll never come home . . . (sob)."

That has always been one of my secret fears. After all, the news is always quick to report the fatalities of hunters who were mistaken for deer. Pulling back my own tears, I allowed my sweet, sensitive son to get up and watch "just a little more T.V." It was 9:45 before he fell asleep that night. The next day at day care my son behaved like a one-eyed lizard with sun stroke.

That night over dinner, Preston and I had "the talk." I told Preston that his bed time was 8:00, and that he had such a bad day at school because he was tired. I also said that Daddy was just fine and "If Daddy were here, he would want you in bed at 8:00, too."

With wide-eyed innocence, Preston said, "Okay, Mommy."

I felt pretty smug. I realized that all Preston needed was for me to be firm and tell him exactly what the rules were.

That night I had Preston bathed and tucked in bed at 7:55. At 7:57, the crying started.

"Cut it out, Preston!" I yelled from the living room. I was determined not to give in tonight. I would not even go back to his room.

At 8:12 the cries had escalated to wails of despair. "Knock it off, Preston," I shouted firmly. Although his screams for Daddy were beginning to wear on my nerves, I was not going to break.

At 8:25 he was bellowing so loudly, I was beginning to worry that the neighbors would call the police and turn me in for child abuse. I walked back to his room to talk with him and was greeted by a puffy, little red face smeared with mucous and tears.

"I muh—muh—miss Daddy," he cried.

I picked him up, feeling a combination of pity and guilt, as well as a sense that I was being conned. I also knew that I had lost the battle.

While pushing back the image of what sort of creature my child would be the next day at school, I started to suggest that we watch "a little T.V." Then the phone rang. It was my husband. With twisted relief I explained to him the situation I had been wrestling with the past three days.

"Put Preston on," he said.

I gave the phone to my son and told him that it was Daddy. Like a sudden cloudburst, the tears sprung from his eyes.

"Daddy," he said, "I miss—yes, Daddy . . . No, Daddy . . . good night, Daddy." Then Preston handed me the phone and scurried to bed.

Stunned, I asked Charles what he had told our son.

"Well," he replied, "I asked him if he knew that I was hunting and that hunting made me happy. He said he did. Then I told him that if I had to come home to make sure he went to bed on time, that I'd be very unhappy, and I asked him if that's what he wanted. He said he didn't, so I told him to go to bed and we said good night."

I learned a lot from that experience about being consistent and the need for a unified front. But I also learned that just because I had worked with adolescents as a counselor, I was not immune from my own child's manipulations. That was a bitter pill to swallow. You see, another part of the kids' job is to keep their parents humble. The ways in which they can pinpoint our feelings of inadequacy as a parent are uncanny. Now, having raised teens of my own, I have learned that children only become more resourceful in their manipulations. Remember, part of growing up is testing parental rules and values.

Rules

If you are re-establishing rules or maybe making consistent rules for the first time, expect things to get worse before they get better. Don't forget that it is our kids' job to test us. If they sense that you are making some changes, they will need to do some limit-pushing to see if these rules are real.

I don't like to talk in terms of absolutes or give a lot of advice because life isn't that black and white. But I have found from my own experience and from the stories of others that it isn't wise to "bluff'" kids or threaten to do things that we aren't prepared to carry through. If our kids test us on a bluff we can't follow through with, we are sure to lose our credibility.

I remember one mother telling me that when her thirteen-year-old son continued to break curfew, she threatened to lock him out of the house. "He was an hour late so I locked the door," she told me. "It was winter and it was bitterly cold. When he finally came home, I could see him standing outside with no boots and no hat and no mittens, because you know it's not 'cool' to let your friends see you all bundled up, and he was all red and shivering and hopping and bopping from foot to foot. What could I do? I couldn't let him freeze to death. I had to let him in, and I knew that he was just laughing inside."

Experimentation and Early Intervention

Once a kid has established an abusive relationship with chemicals, focusing on being a good role model, getting to know the child, and setting consistent rules with reasonable consequences probably won't be enough. If we think our kids are in trouble with drugs, it's time to get professional, objective help. But there is a lot we can do before it gets to that point. Please remember, though, there is no magic formula to keep kids off drugs. However, there are many ways parents can make it uncomfortable, at the least, for their children to pursue an ongoing relationship with chemicals. Most kids will at least try drinking or drugs before they graduate from high school. Before this happens, it is important that we talk with our kids about our rules surrounding the use of mood-altering substances. Abstinence until they are older is probably the best way to go. Some studies show that if you wait until the age of twenty-four before using chemicals, your chances of becoming dependent are slim. We all know that this may not be realistic. I think it's good to discuss with kids not only what our expectations are surrounding chemical use—like "don't do it"—but also what our expectations are if they find themselves in a situation where they are with people who are using or if they are using themselves. S.A.D.D. (Students Against Drunk Driving) has endorsed contracts which will allow a using teenager to call home for a ride, no matter what time, with no questions asked.

As a prevention tool this kind of contract has considerable merit. It makes the issue of chemical use an open subject within the family. When there is openness, there is opportunity to have honest discussions about limits as well as concerns of both parents and children. Deception and dishonesty are the forerunners of a chemical abuse problem. It is also important to discuss with children what, if any, consequences we will impose if they do use chemicals. We also need to consider whether the consequences will be different if they are honest with us or if they are caught lying.

There really is no rule to follow when determining what your expectations are. But the ability to discuss these issues and establish reasonable rules and consequences may be more important than the rules themselves. If you are having trouble settling on limits that the family can live with, I would encourage you to seek the help of a mediator. A good mediator could be a drug or school counselor, teacher, clergy member, social worker, a sponsor from a twelve-step group, or someone else who has familiarity with chemically related issues and/or family support.

Dee

I had a cousin who was killed while driving drunk. It really shook up my family. Up until that time we never talked much about alcohol or drugs or stuff like that. About a month later, my parents said that we were going to talk with this woman from my church. They didn't say what we were going to talk about. When we got there I was surprised to find that we were going to talk about drinking and me.

At first I was pretty pissed off. I guess I was scared, too, because I had been to a couple of parties where people were drinking and I'd had a few drinks myself. My parents said they thought I was at the age where I might start experimenting with alcohol or drugs and they wanted us to be able to talk about it. I wasn't going to tell them anything, but then this lady started talking about my cousin and his death. It turned out that she had lost a kid that way, too. Now she works with other kids and families in some kind of program at the church.

Anyway, I did tell my parents that I had been to a few parties and we talked about it. My parents were pretty cool about it. They said that they didn't want me to lie about it if I did use. We wrote up this contract about drinking and driving and some other rules, too. I agreed to be honest with them about my drinking and stuff and they agreed not to spaz out if I did drink.

Then there was a part where I would agree to an assessment if I lied or broke other parts of the contract, or if something serious happened because of my use. I was pretty skeptical that this thing would work. But now it's been two years, and I'm seventeen. For the most part it seems like it helped us. I found out that I could really talk with my folks about some pretty hard things and that they would listen. There were a couple of times when I didn't hold up my end of the bargain and they were upset. But it all worked out. I even think it's helped to make us closer in other ways, too. I've tried alcohol and pot, but there are other things in my life that are more important. My relationship with my parents is one. I have a lot of years ahead of me. I guess partying can wait for now.

When Parents "Just Say No"

When it comes to setting and enforcing limits, a family is not a democracy. Parents set the rules. Another parenting job is to decide when a line has been crossed and then to decide what will be done about it.

Knowing just when or how to intervene in our children's experimentation can be a ticklish subject. Although we can't do anything to guarantee that our children won't have a problem with drugs, we do know when we become uncomfortable with their using pattern.

What may be acceptable for one child may not be acceptable for another. There are no hard and fast rules. But we may have a lower tolerance for experimentation by high-risk children than we would if our children seemed fairly stable in their self-esteem and showed good judgment and open communication skills.

Beverly

I was much more tolerant of my older boy, Jim, experimenting with alcohol than I was with Billy. They are eight years apart and Jim was grown before Billy was even a teenager. Jim tried drinking along with the other guys on his team. He was a pretty popular kid and captain of the basketball team. He got into a few scrapes where we had to come down on him, but he seemed to pull himself out if it and do all right.

I worry more about Billy. He's a great kid, but he has some learning disabilities, and school has always been hard for him. It doesn't help that his older brother was a star, either. Billy is more insecure and his feelings are easily hurt. He's kind of shy, too, and has gotten in trouble a few times because he's done things "on dares" or just to go along with the other kids. Last year his dad was killed in a car accident. My limits with Billy are stricter than they were for Jim when he was fifteen. I know Billy resents me for that, but I have to do what feels right.

Don't underestimate trusting your instincts as a parent. Sometimes rules aren't fair—and our kids will be the first ones to point that out. It is crucial to make decisions that feel good deep inside, as opposed to making decisions that will win popularity contests with our children.

Once we have become uncomfortable with our children's use—for whatever reason—that is the time to intervene. I wish I had a nickel for every time I have heard a parent say, "I just don't know if I have the right to do anything because I don't have a lot of proof. All I have is how I feel." Well, that's enough.

Another part of our job description as parents is to intervene when we think it's necessary. That's what a parent is supposed to do. If this sounds like a lot of work, you're right, it is. And sometimes it can feel pretty overwhelming—especially if you have more than one child. If you have a job, are a single parent, have more than one child, or are dealing with other personal problems, it can get to be too much for one person to handle alone. If you are feeling overwhelmed, it is because you are overwhelmed. When your kids feel conflict at home, they talk about you to their friends. I think that they have the right idea. The supportive ear of a friend or group may be crucial to you so that you don't find yourself feeling isolated or alone.

Not having all the answers while you are trying to juggle all the responsibility can be a tough job. We're bound to make some mistakes along the way. This is an occupational hazard. Along with the mistakes comes self-doubt. And kids seem to be able to tell instinctively when parental power is beginning to waiver.

A friend of mine and his wife were struggling with establishing rules. They tried a number of different approaches: no rules, lenient and very flexible rules with limited consequences, and rigid rules with harsh consequences. With each approach his kids tested the limits as far as they could. He told me that his kids had become unusually surly and he had been particularly edgy. "I tried to be reasonable by warning them about the consequences if their behaviors continued, but they were relentless," he said. "Then one day Joe broke Rachel's 'village of the future' that she was making for school. She was crying, he was laughing, and I guess I snapped. I told Joe that he couldn't go on the class ski trip that was coming up. I knew it was too harsh, but at the same time I knew that if I didn't follow through it would be just one more time I had given a consequence that I didn't back up. I went for a long walk to think about it, and to get away from it for a while. I decided that Joe would have other ski trips, one was even later in the month, and that it would probably be worse in the long run if I did anything right now to make my credibility shakier that it already was. When I returned home, I apologized to Joe for being so harsh. But then I told him that this time he'd have to live with a harsh consequence because not only did I need him to take me seriously, I needed to take myself seriously. He's been pouting ever since, but I can handle that."

I know from my own experience as a mother, there are times when I wouldn't win any popularity contests. But being popular isn't what it takes to raise a child today. Sometimes parents have to make decisions that kids don't like. Sometimes when it would be easier or more fun to be "soft" or give in, we need to be tough. Kids need limits. They don't necessarily like limits, but they need them. Part of our job as parents is to set and enforce those limits. We do this to keep our kids safe and to prepare them for life as adults. Being to class on time is good practice for being to work on time. Learning about priorities and developing into responsible, thoughtful adults is an important part of growing up.

Is There Hope?

I wish I had some magic formula to give to parents so they can battle the adolescent drug problem. But as I said from the beginning, there is no such formula.

Healing can happen for families. It starts when parents decide not only that they want a better life for their kids, but that they want a better life for themselves.

The most powerful gift parents can give their kids is to be happy with themselves. If circumstances in your home are causing your unhappiness, there are things you can do to change them. You may not be able to change your child, but you can change your expectations for acceptable behavior from that child.

Yes, it is tough to make these changes, but change does work. The stories in this book are about families involved in a metamorphosis. Sometimes their stories are painful and frustrating—but often new insights can be uncomfortable. Feeling bad doesn't necessarily mean you are doing badly. Sometimes feeling bad has to happen so you will know what to change. If you're not sure how to make these changes, find other families who have shared a similar struggle. The wisdom you will gain is priceless.

I remember when a former client returned to visit me three years after he had been in treatment. He told me that when he left treatment, he didn't stay straight.

"I went back to using after three months,"

he said. "But I wasn't the same. I felt bad about it because of what I learned in treatment. But it was my family who really got to me. It was like they got smarter! They were harder to fool and they followed through with consequences when I screwed up."

He went on to tell me that after two more treatments, his family was ready to kick him out of the house.

"That's when it hit me," he said. "They'd gotten better without me and I didn't want to lose them. I decided I was pretty lucky to have them, and that I had better do something to keep them."

People recover at their own rate. Although there is little you can do to make it "easy" for your child to recover, the changes you make in your own life will make it uncomfortable for your kid if he or she does not change.

And that is a positive start.